For the Love of Children

A Realistic Approach to Raising Your Child

Edward E. Ford
and
Steven Englund

EDWARD E. FORD
SCOTTSDALE, ARIZONA
1986

*For my daughters: Dorothy, Terry, and Mary Ellen
and my sons: John, Nelson, Joseph, Thomas, and Luke.*

*For Steven Castle, Lucie Schaff, Toby Odell, and
Kirby Kotler.*

Special Acknowledgment

For the more than eight years that I have worked with Dr. William Glasser as my friend and colleague, I have been intimately exposed to his creative thinking. Not only have I applied the ideas of Reality Therapy in my work, but I have found them valuable in my personal and family life as well. It follows naturally, therefore, that Dr. Glasser's ideas are interwoven into this book in many places as they were in my previous books. Specifically, I wish to acknowledge that he introduced me to some of the key ideas in Chapters One, Two, and Four—the concepts of strength and weakness, the choice of feelings and behavior, and the danger of excessive television-viewing for the young.

Edward E. Ford

Contents

Preface xi

PART I *Children Today: Anatomy of the Problem*
 Chapter 1 Strength 3
 Chapter 2 Choices 22

PART II *The Way Back*
 Chapter 3 Love 43
 Chapter 4 Responsibility 60
 Chapter 5 Discipline 79
 Chapter 6 Work 91
 Chapter 7 Play 108
 Chapter 8 Faith 126

PART III *Hope*
 Chapter 9 Children? 143

Bibliography 151

Preface

This book has turned out to be a collaboration in the fullest sense of the word, but it did not begin that way. Originally the book was intended to develop Ed Ford's ideas about child-raising in the prose of Steve Englund. Early on, however, both men discovered a concurrence of ideas and fruitfulness of reasoning in tandem that ultimately led to a completely coauthored work—a book which we hope is different from, and better than, the one originally intended, precisely because it issued from a process of rapport and self-transcendence on the part of the two authors. If we have adopted the vertical pronoun—I—throughout the book (with one exception in the chapter on faith), this is for convenience and brevity. In truth, however, that "I" represents the two of us and is also, by the way, larger than the sum of its parts.

As parent, Ed has of course made many mistakes in his attempt to raise eight children. His understanding of what creates strength and weakness in young people emerged gradually from a slow process of trial and error. And this process continues today.

It is always difficult for authors to write the "thank yous" to the people who have helped them. We wish to single out our editor at Doubleday, Charles Priester—who could with justification be included in the authorship of this book. Charlie's painstaking, tireless devotion to editing the book brought it successfully through what Solzhenitsyn called "the realm of the Final Inch."

Also, the authors wish to thank M. Holmes Hartshorne, Professor of Philosophy and Religion at Colgate University, who gave to our chapter on faith the same care and intelligence he put into educating Steve.

Unfortunately, these men may only be thanked; they cannot carry any of the burden of the mistakes, omissions, or other misdeeds we may have committed in our book.

Thanks, too, to our special readers, Hester Ford, Father Joseph Lucas, Larry Ceplair, Don Fausel, and our devoted typist-reader, Frances Rehm.

Edward E. Ford
Steven Englund
Scottsdale, Arizona

> The soul of a child, as it reaches out
> toward understanding, has need of the treasures
> accumulated by the human species through
> the centuries.

Simone Weil, *The Need for Roots*

PART I

Children Today: Anatomy of the Problem

CHAPTER 1

Strength

There was a child went forth every day
and the first object he look'd upon, that object
    he became
and that object became part of him for the day
    or a certain part of the day
or for many years or stretching cycles of years.

Walt Whitman

This is a book about creating strength in young people from
infancy through adolescence. There are innumerable kinds of
strength, of course, and we are concerned with many of them—
moral, spiritual, intellectual strength. But what it finally comes
down to is the sort of integrative and integrated strengh of
character which the Greeks associated with the harmony of
developed mind, body, and soul. Harmony in this sense means
wholeness. We are an age of specialists, of breakers-down and
compartmentalizers. This approach may serve a useful function in technology, but when it is applied to human life, the
consequences are unfortunate. A great deal is lost in terms of
the vision, the purpose, and the potential of life. The strength
we are concerned with in this book, then, is the strength that
comes from fullness of life. The ancient Greeks, our cultural
and intellectual forebears, had a word for such strength. They

called it *arete*—which meant simply "excellence" in *all* the ways mankind can attain excellence: morally, intellectually, spiritually, physically, practically.

Strength in this complete sense is not only what sees a person through the unavoidable tragedies, defeats, and stresses of life—what we could call courage, or coping strength; it is also a set of patterns of living which ensure that the person fulfills all of his potential in life, that he is human in the widest, highest meaning of the word. For life is not only, not even mainly, a question of muddling through —though there are increasingly large amounts of muddling to do. It is *still,* as it always was, an opportunity for joy, wholeness, transcendence.

Strength, in the sense of both courage and fulfillment, is not easily or rapidly learned. Indeed it may take a lifetime to acquire. The sources and varieties of strength are many: love, responsibility, work, discipline, play, faith, to name the several sources which to me seem fundamental. And yet their position in our society is precarious. These building blocks of strength have been sapped at their core by the corrosive effects of a myriad of agents and institutions in our society. They have been turned into caricatures of themselves, have been corrupted or repressed or disguised, and any serious attempt to revitalize these strengths must first unearth and cleanse them from the accumulated muck of the media's and the culture's abuse. This will not happen easily or quickly, but what is equally true is that the child who learns and assimilates the real meaning and expression of love, responsibility, discipline, work, play, and faith will have nothing to fear, and very much to anticipate, in life.

The process of this learning and assimilation is the crux of this book. To that end, although this is a book about young people, it must concentrate on adults—parents, teachers, counselors, friends—who care about, and who form, young people; for they are the examples from whose words and actions children learn strength.

We are essentially *social beings,* as we have learned from philosophers Aristotle through Rousseau, and although it is fashionable to stress the animal or natural side of man, the kinds of strength this book seeks to revive and restore are the rational, moral, and spiritual qualities unique to man-as-being in company with his fellow beings. Strength, though it may occasionally be cultivated and demonstrated in solitude, is fundamentally a social attribute. Ultimately it is learned only from examples of strength shown by people who care about us, the people whom social scientists call our "significant others." We may acquire strength throughout our lives, but the critical time is during infancy, childhood, and youth; and in those years the decisive teacher-demonstrator of strength is the parents.

Ever since the dawn of human history, mankind has acculturated himself and his young to the necessary social skills of survival by the trial and error, the effort and experiences *of interaction* with other people. In our day, unfortunately, it seems we have lost touch with the process (not to mention the values) whereby strength is created and passed on to our young. The social habits and institutions of interaction are becoming increasingly trivialized or superficial; too often, they are simply nonexistent. And the consequences are omnipresent. *Psychology Today* in its cover story of November 1976 reported that parent "training" and "effectiveness" programs are growing by leaps and bounds in this country, attesting to parents' growing inability and need to develop satisfying relationships with their children. The Parent Involvement Program (P.I.P.), based on William Glasser's Reality Therapy, is one such fast-growing course offered parents throughout the country. Another is P.E.T. (Parent Effectiveness Training), which is the largest—in the few years since its inception, it has taught some 8,000 instructors and over a quarter of a million parents about communication, conflict resolution, and involvement with their children.

It is not only parents who are in need either. I have given

workshops in over sixty school districts in the past three years, and I keep hearing the same refrains from teachers: "My students don't listen." "They can't tolerate frustration." "They fight more." "They can't express themselves verbally or in writing." "They don't know how to think."

Let's not delude and console ourselves with the reassurance that young people are always, in any era, obstreperous and difficult. The statistics of alcoholism and alcohol use, of drug addiction and use, of criminal violence and arrests among today's young, even the very young, are appalling.

Over the past fifteen years, FBI reports show that arrests of minors (under eighteen) increased nearly 300 per cent for violent crimes, over 500 per cent for drunken driving, 191 per cent for other liquor law violations, and an earth-shaking 4,400 per cent for violations of narcotics laws. Nearly two million children under eighteen were arrested in the United States last year.[1]

However alarming the upswing of criminal behavior among youth, most children still manage to grow up without police records. How many, though, have avoided the consequences of a lack of a strength-creating, strength-enhancing relationship with their parents and other adults? The daily experience of living with the non-criminal youth of today means much more than statistics of social pathology. In offering the following composite portrait of the worst aspects of the "new" child, I am fully aware that it could be considered a caricature, that of course it doesn't depict completely or fairly all there is to children. Nonetheless, I feel it illuminates the darker underside of the truth about vast numbers of young people today and therefore needs to be said.

The mark of the new child is his lack of curiosity, of excitement, for learning and being active—from playing with tinker

[1] National Council on Crime and Delinquency, Supplement in the New York *Times* magazine, Summer 1976. Telephone interview with FBI headquarters spokesman in Washington, D.C. National Institute on Alcoholism spokesman in Phoenix, Arizona.

toys to practicing the violin to holding a conversation. The mark of the new child is his pervasive materialism, which shows little concern for other people's property or the value of his own, which treats people and playmates like possessions, and possessions like commodities to be replaced as fast as they are worn out or lost.

The new child stands hip-deep in an irrational narcissism quite different from the instinctual self-centeredness of children of other eras, because he thrives on an inadequate self-identity and blind self-indulgence that reject concern for human interdependence. The identifying characteristic of the new child is his immersion in his own weakened self and in the electronic extensions of that self furnished by Sony, RCA, and Honda. The child's lack of involvement with people, even his own parents, leads to the parents' utter lack of control over their child. As a result, the children are not open to discipline, nor even responsive for very long to punishment . . . only to permissiveness and protective insulation.

The mark of the new child is his emotional precocity, so impressive at first glance, until one becomes aware that it marks an underlying insensitivity and a subtle skill at manipulating other people's emotions, coupled with a desperate but totally unconscious need for true love and human interaction. This child of the media is not unemotional or invulnerable, but his emotions are shallow, calculating, and self-centered.

Finally, the mark of the new child is his inability to cope with frustration and stress—with all those demands and challenges, setbacks and problems that life invariably throws in the path of human beings. The new child's instant recourse is to act out, to blame others, to elude responsibility, to drop out, to take the easy road of avoidance, addiction, apathy.

Obviously these descriptions of contemporary youth do not apply to everybody in our society under the age of twenty-one. The words are stark and hard; they are intended to reflect the reality underneath the statistics, which are themselves alarming. We have a problem on our hands of our own making, and that problem is weakness. Our young people, *in ever increasing numbers,* are showing signs of severe character weakness— escapism, excessive drinking, drug abuse, criminality, violence, materialism, narcissism, are the most conspicuous examples—which testify to their inability to cope and grow and derive fulfillment from life.

This weakness is born of passivity. It is not so much a specific ailment as the source of many different woes and dissatisfactions. In an age such as ours—of increasing, but conflicting expectations; of widening discrepancy between education and training, and the availability of jobs; of rapid, stress-producing change; of the emotional and physical stress of competition, criticism, and the omnipresent threats of war, terrorism, ecological imbalance, loneliness, and the disintegration of traditional values; and, finally, of the increasing availability of debilitating nostrums (both ideological and pharmacological)—there is a greater need than ever for *the strength to cope,* the strength which expresses itself as courage, flexibility, centeredness, resourcefulness, and self-reliance.

Coping strength is quite simply confidence in your ability to figure out what to do when you don't know what to do. It is only one aspect, perhaps the lesser, of the character strength which flows from, and creates, a full human life. But under the current circumstances of our society, coping is the best place to begin for many young people. For only through successful coping will they, or we, surmount the distracting difficulties of life, and then make contact with the greater, more distant horizons of joy, wholeness, and transcendence to which coping strength leads. Strength is unitary, finally, and the paths to acquiring its coping aspect are the same paths that will lead to the farthest pastures. The difficulty lies in making young people aware of what they *could* be, of what life *could* be, and then showing and teaching them how to begin realizing that potential. Instead, we continue to manufacture in ourselves and our young the weakness of apathy, illusion, escapism, irresponsibility, narcissism, dependence.

Now more than ever, we need strength; yet, less than ever before, are we producing it in our children.

Social critics have been correct to enumerate the "larger causes" of our own and our children's weakness—pervasive ideological and cultural propaganda; unjust distribution of wealth and power; over-dependent parent-child relations in the post-industrial nuclear family; political corruption and its negative conditioning effects on young people; inadequate and overcrowded schools; insufficient recreational facilities, etc. But in a practical book intended to lend a helping hand, the brilliant exposition of "larger causes" is only marginally useful, unless the message to be conveyed is one of passive hopelessness. Instead, I would like to focus with some intensity on one particular, omnipresent source of human weakness which is within our purview to change.

From the mythic Pied Piper of Hamelin and the Children's Crusade of the twelfth century to the Hitler Youth and today's "Moonies," young people have occasionally been victimized by the leadership of their elders. Misleading the young, however, is not only confined to such unusual, faraway examples as these. For if the Hitler youth and the followers of Rev. Sun Myung Moon seem far-fetched, let us consider a victimization of young people that is much closer to home, my home and yours. Never has an *entire* generation of children been so transfixed with an enfeebling enchantment as post-1955 youth's obsession with electronic media, particularly the talking pictures of the black box: TV.

The main problem with television is *not*, finally, the advertising, *not* the programing, *not* the violence on the tube (hateful as these things are), but rather *the wasted value of the hours upon hours which the child spends away from strength-building contact with other people*. We are not the first to sound this alarm. The noted child psychologist Urie Bronfenbrenner said in a speech delivered in 1971: "The primary danger of the television screen lies not so much in the behavior it produces as the behavior it prevents. . . . Turning on the television set can turn off the process that transforms children into people."

The social skills of getting along, expressing oneself, listening, and playing satisfyingly, are all learned primarily at home in the early years. Similarly, the foundations of intellectual skills and creativity are laid and nourished in important ways in the child's home life. If one doesn't acquire these intellectual and social skills, and learn them in depth and with fluency, then no matter how much he may superficially appear to be an adult in terms of speech, dress, and age, the moment the stresses of life and the demands of social intercourse mount, or become complex, he will betray his inner fissures and weaknesses with violence, withdrawal, inflexibility, or any number of other unfortunate "choices" (see Chapter 2). He will not know from experience what to do when school gets hard or he loses his job, or his marriage starts to fall apart, or he feels bored, or his life becomes generally unsatisfying.

The major social strengths of life—play, work, love, faith—will be relatively strange lands for the TV-weakened child, experiences he has tasted only vicariously, at secondhand, or partially. He will in a truly lamentable sense, remain something of a stranger to the species and the promise of his human birth. And the final twist is, he won't know these things until it is very late. Indeed he may never learn them, but instead will simply make do with the halfway mechanisms, surrogates, and material crutches of an affluent society. Like a baby who is born blind, the generation of the media child may never discover what it is missing, though it constantly feels the dull inexplicable ache of emptiness.

The post-1955 generation is the first wave of young people in the history of the world to be systematically deprived of most of their socializing time. This cannot help but have a severely devitalizing impact upon them. To expect them at high school or college age suddenly to blossom into functioning and articulate adults, after fourteen or fifteen years of passive staring, would be like tying the legs of a child until he is twelve and then asking him to run a foot race. The only way you learn to run is by running, to talk by talking, to handle the stresses and demands of human interaction by engaging in it from the earliest age, and developing, honing, improving these social skills over the years of childhood and youth.

I do not mean to load upon excessive television-viewing the entire burden of all of the problems of young people—nor even rule out the possibility that TV-itis is itself symptomatic of some greater, underlying sickness in our society. But from my perspective of twenty-five years as father, teacher, counselor, therapist, consultant, and writer, I see excessive TV-viewing as the singular hallmark or symbol of the weakness I spoke of earlier—the most decisive and basic element in the cocktail of causes contributing to youth's inability to cope.

The problem of too much TV was visible as early as 1956 in *The Man in the Gray Flannel Suit*. The movie starred Gregory Peck, who played the part of a corporate executive so caught up in his job and career that he has little time for his family. An important scene in the film shows Peck coming home late on the train one evening to his house in the suburbs. His two children are lying in their pajamas on the floor in front of the television, too mesmerized to take much account of their father, who peers at them from the doorway behind. I wonder how many of us who saw that film then suspected that twenty years later, Nielsen surveys would show that most young children would be seeing a good deal more of the tube than of their fathers. In any event, *The Man in the Gray Flannel Suit* was a harbinger of things to come.

Today, 97 per cent of all U.S. households have at least one television set, and 43 per cent have two or more sets. The average American family now logs over six hours a day in front of the tube, while the individual viewer watches for four hours.[2] According to a 1974 Gallup survey, TV-watching

[2] A. C. Nielsen.

remains this country's most popular pastime; 46 per cent of all persons interviewed said that TV is their favorite evening entertainment. This compares with 14 per cent who preferred reading, 10 per cent who liked staying at home talking with the family, and 8 per cent who chose to spend time with a friend.

The average high school graduate in this country has spent 11,000 hours in the classroom, but will have watched almost twice that many hours of TV, and been exposed to 350,000 commercials and 18,000 murders. Time spent before the tube varies with a child's age. The grand trophy of TV-itis goes to preschoolers. At an age, from two to six years, which all educators and psychologists agree is utterly crucial and decisive in a child's development, the average preschooler watches TV (or is in a home where the set is turned on) fifty-three hours per week—or about eight hours a day.[3] I find that statistic hair-raising. It's miraculous to me that these youngsters ever grow up at all.

Television is the first, most classic means of teaching a generation of children that the way to "feel good" need not entail any work; thus, it originates and cultivates the child's ongoing need for stimulation without providing any room for growth. Television creates the pattern of sense bombardment which later on, when the child becomes a teen-ager, requires the most sophisticated technology of our gadget-obsessed society for its fulfillment. Headphones and stereos, tape decks and electronically hyped-up instruments, portable radios and cassettes, all try to fill with noise the void that television-watching created in the life of the youngster, as if somehow immersion in sheer decibels could drown out the need for love and worth.

New York magazine recently devoted an entire issue[4] to the glories of the electronic media under the subtitle "Last Year

[3] "The Television Era" by Joann S. Lublin, *Wall Street Journal* series on TV, October 1976.

[4] *New York* magazine, April 1976.

the Family Room, This Year the Media Room". The richly illustrated articles inside the magazine constituted a celebration
of media technology, providing the reader in Sears-catalogue
fashion with the latest, most expensive ways of tuning in and
dropping out: e.g., the Multi-Track Magnetics, PH-16 projector, the McIntosh C28 preamplifier, the Shintron 300 console,
the Chromaton 14 (for creating exotic designs on your TV
screen), and so forth. (The final item of a long list included a
Reuter News Report teleprinter for $250. Somehow one won-
ders if the people who acquire these gadgets would be very
psyched up about getting regular printouts from an English
news service.)

The writer of one of the stories in this issue rounded up and
interviewed some of the "media freaks" on the New York
scene. I was especially appalled by the report of one young
couple in their proud tenth month of owning the Advent
Video-Beam TV projector and its seven-foot diagonal screen
(described as "this month's hot item," costing a mere $3,995).
The woman and her boyfriend happily admit to spending
fewer nights out—more company, *but less* conversation. And
they love it. "It's like living in the best movie theater. The only
problem is when you turn off the picture, *there's an empty
feeling*—like the movie's over and you should clear out." (My
emphasis.) As a result of these feelings of "emptiness," the
couple never turn the set off. They even watch commercials
avidly. Having said all this, the couple realized that perhaps
people would get "the wrong idea," so they hastened to remind
the *New York* reporter that "even though the big picture
suppresses talk," Schaffer (the boyfriend) is also an amateur
radio operator who communicates with two hundred coun-
tries. Still, adds Schaffer, all he talks about with other ham
radio operators "is the weather."

I am wondering if the previous example needs any explanation. If the reader of this book doesn't see the internal waste-
land which the comments and contraptions of these people
betoken, then he or she probably won't get much out of this

book anyway. The unspoken faith in technology, underwritten and illustrated by the two devotees interviewed by *New York,* somehow maintains that the expense and novelty of a gadget will mitigate the harmfulness of its impact. Having very likely spent their youth in front of the tube, these upper-class Americans know no better way to express their "maturity" and "adulthood" than to turn their home into one giant "media room." Their social and personal lives revolve around the grotesquerie of an electronically expanded TV set.

The people who spoke of their media mania in *New York* are probably beyond the likelihood of heeding this book. So, unfortunately, are their children. I am interested, therefore, in reaching parents, counselors, teachers, therapists—*any* adults, in fact—who take the problem of our weakened young seriously.

The effects of this weakness are ubiquitous, not only in the lives of our children, but more importantly when they reach majority. A Colorado University professor of business and management recently conducted a study of the job turnover among young people in business. Young people have trouble keeping a job, let alone advancing to a higher level, because they expect immediate gratification in the form of quick promotions and excitement. If they don't get them, they leave. Said the professor: "Kids are being conditioned by television to think that any problem can be resolved in a half hour." They have very little imagination, flexibility, or "ability to cope with stress in the marketplace." The professor is concerned, understandably, with the attitude-conditioning effect of TV programs. What he overlooks, like many researchers, is the more critical fact that no matter what programing is flickering on the screen in front of children for four to six hours a day, children can't afford that much time *away from* the experiences and activities which teach the basic social, intellectual, and physical skills of human life.

The alternative to too much television-viewing can be seen most dramatically in a study conducted by a Harvard University educational psychologist, Burton L. White.[5] He discovered that the brightest, happiest, most charming and socially adept children spend their earliest years in remarkably similar ways. They listen to, and participate in, adult conversation; they roam freely around their homes; and they spend a lot of time just exploring objects. The key seems to be the time that attentive, responsive parents spend with their children—parents who are on hand and enthusiastic, whether their youngsters want help, comfort, or simply a chance to share discoveries. The preschoolers also have frequent opportunity to engage in simple conversation with their parents, or to overhear adult talk even when they don't understand it. Equally important, the youngsters do a lot of staring at objects (as much as 15 to 20 per cent of their waking time)—a completely different pastime from passively watching television, because it is self-controlled and initiated, uninterrupted, active learning.

The most dramatic illustration of the effects of TV-viewing on children comes from an experiment conducted by *Redbook* magazine with a group of families in New Milford, Connecticut.[6] Approximately fifteen mothers were asked to monitor the shows their children watched, to limit their overall viewing time to one hour a day, and to keep diaries on what changes transpired in their children's behavior and disposition. In case after case the same pattern of results was noted. During the first week of TV dieting, children were cranky and fidgety as if they were experiencing "withdrawal pains." Many parents felt that the absence of the tube was "like losing a valued babysitter."

By the third week of the experiment some remarkable changes were noted. Children who were previously passive, withdrawn, and shy were now reported, by teachers and parents alike, to be showing interest, imagination, and re-

[5] Daniel Q. Haney, "Study Happy Children," Youngstown *Vindicator,* Youngstown, Ohio, February 3, 1976.
[6] Claire Safran, "How TV Changes Children," *Redbook* magazine, November 1976, pp. 88–97.

sourcefulness. Where previously they had been nervous and anxious, they now acted calmly and in a more relaxed manner. Parents and children were spending much more time together and the quality of that time was heightened. Talking, reading, and playing blossomed; games were hauled out of closets or invented, and music, paints, paste, blocks, and clay were resurrected. Other longer-term benefits accrued: grades went up, children and parents got along better, and children cleaned their rooms more often.

In sum, these youngsters derived strength and growth from the *rich social experience* their parents provided, which necessarily *precluded too much exposure to the television set*. As we will see in later chapters of this book, the time parents spend actively with their children is the surest index of parental love. Any parent—even one with limited time for his children—can control the hours his sons and daughters watch TV and can maximize the impact of the social interaction he has with them. If this book does nothing else, I hope it will teach all parents, rich or poor, some of the things they can do to build strength in their media-weakened offspring.

I have stressed raw viewing time as the crucial gradient in television's negative effect, but I'd also like to say a word about the content of programing and commercial advertising and its conditioning impact upon children's attitudes and expectations. If I do not stress this overly, however, it is because so much has already been written in popular and scientific literature to awaken people to the unfortunate consequences of violence, mindlessness, materialism, etc. in TV programing. The larger point I have tried to make is that even if commercials were banned from television and educational, moral, or aesthetic goals strictly governed programing, it would still be a calamitous mistake to allow young people to watch TV anywhere near as much as they currently do. Passive viewing for such long periods of time takes too many hours away from those that children should be spending in active, strength-building pursuits.

The 350,000 commercials which the average young person will have watched on TV by the time he or she is eighteen years old, contribute to the creation of frenetic, utterly false needs. These needs play upon a young person's desire to be happy, always a sacred aspiration in an identity-oriented society like ours, but they equate happiness with such illusions and ephemera (youth, popularity, breath, sugared cereal, novel toys, clean armpits, tasty junkfood) that the viewer loses all sense of real values.

Considering the weakened character that excessive TV-viewing creates in the first place, it is small wonder that a child's, especially a preschooler's, resistance to the philosophy of life promulgated by commercial advertising is critically low. Constant reminders of one's inadequacy and potential unpopularity, juxtaposed with the blessed assurance that fast relief can be had with Product X, increase the illusion and ultimately, when Product X doesn't work, the frustration.

Together with the content of most children's and adult's network programing, commercial advertising fosters an instant-cure mentality which expects life to be simple and fun-filled, and problems of all sorts to be soluble in a variety of technological, pharmacological, and ideological confections. Underlying this mentality, however, is an unconscious substream of inadequacy and pain—stemming from weakness, from the absence of meaningful feelings of love and worth—which the child can never manage to permanently alter, but only relieve or drown out by immersion in more and more TV, or loud music, or, eventually in alcohol, dope, and crime.

If commercials offer drugs, gadgets, cosmetic-hygienic products, and junkfood as the classic "ways out" of problems, TV programing by and large offers unalloyed, massive doses of violence. As we say, the statistics of crime and arrest among the young are awesome. In fact, it is now generally agreed that a *direct causal relationship* exists between the violence of television programing and the violence of young people (and adults) in their daily lives. Even leading network executives now publicly concede, in the words of Julian Goodman (Chairman of the Board of NBC), "that the Surgeon General's study ["Television and Social Behavior" (1972)] told us more than we had ever known before about the relationship between viewing violence on television and subsequent behavior," and that "that relationship is now generally recognized."

As the need for love and worth mount in the TV-weakened child, with no related increase in his social skills and capacities for creating these experiences for himself, the temptation to "act out"—i.e., to act violently and/or criminally—becomes a logical and sometimes irresistible recourse. What better way to gain attention, one that works 100 per cent of the time, than to cause yourself or someone else pain? Acting out is thus the weak child's (or adult's) surrogate for love, in much the same way as stealing and crime are his replacements for worth.

I don't wish to dwell on violence. It is too established a topic and *cause célèbre* to require more space here. In conclusion, however, I would like to reiterate that *commercial advertising and network programing are critical issues only because we allow ourselves and our children such excessive amounts of time in front of the TV set*. The weakness that immoderate television-viewing creates in young people is what makes them vulnerable to the ravages of advertising and of violent or fatuous programing. Strong children and adults would have nothing to fear from profit-transfixed minds of TV executives who, even when they agree with psychologists that programing is harmful, do nothing to alter it, because "violence pays." It wouldn't matter, because strength of mind and character on the part of TV-viewers could compensate for idiocy on the tube. But strength is precisely what is sapped away, or never developed in the first place, when strength-building time is devoted to passively staring at the black box.

The doubtful reader may still feel that I have been too reductionistic in blaming so many of our children's foibles and shortcomings on excessive exposure to the electronic media, particularly television. What about all those "larger causes" we mentioned earlier? Aren't they at least as responsible as too much TV for the delinquency, superficiality, and diminished coping strength in youth?

Well, yes, I think they are partly responsible. I'd be foolish to think otherwise. But I also think that there is very little that we, as individuals with families, are able to do right now about these factors—all of which have been mulled over endlessly in both popular and highbrow literature. Don't get me wrong—I'm all for top-level social analysis, and I strongly favor collective action toward improving society. But I'm also realistic about the likelihood of anything happening in the near future to alter fundamentally the state of things.

Meanwhile, the anguish and indecision over what to do about raising our children is with us daily—exacerbated by the realization that heretofore we have been doing an inadequate job. So, in addition to hoping for and working toward general improvements and alterations in the structure and functioning of our society, I'd like to offer a healing, helping word to parents who want to know what to do *here and now* for their children.

And here and now, excessive television is *a key problem* which we damn well *can do* something about. More than almost anything else, it bears a direct responsibility for planting seeds of weakness and inadequacy that will later sprout into all manner of unwanted, parasitic, unlovely blossoms. So if you ask me, "What do we do to build strength in our young people?", I would say, read the rest of this book and act on its advice. Any book which seeks to offer ways to rehabilitate drug addicts or alcoholics must necessarily commence with the injunction to stop taking narcotics and drinking liquor. Similarly, a book about filling the media-created void of weakness in our children with varieties of strength (love, responsibility, discipline, work, play, faith) has to begin by insisting that the concerned parent cut back and control *his own and his children's time* in front of the TV screen.

What you, the parents, do (especially if you are willing to spend time with your children) has more impact on them than television has. This said, limit the amount you and your kids watch TV to one hour, as suggested in the *Redbook* experiment, and not one second more. In the TV time now available to your family, encourage the young people to watch "good" programs with you, and occasionally take time to discuss with them the worth or worthlessness of what you are watching. As for commercial advertisements, simply turn off the sound. Every now and then take time to remind your children and yourself of the deceptive techniques and debilitating impact of TV commercials. More important than sermons and discussions, however, are actions. Don't buy the pills, drugs, ointments, sprays, junkfood, alcohol, and useless-but-expensive gadgets which are endlessly paraded before our eyes in thirty-second and one-minute spots.

With this as a start, then, let's move on to the myriad other actions and choices facing the parent and, in turn, the child who have strength and wholeness as their goal.

The remaining chapters follow in a carefully chosen order. To begin with, it seems crucial to me to examine the unfortunate choices that young people may make in the absence of strength and driven by the need to escape the pain of stress and failure. Like all the problems and difficulties parents and children face, the consequences of these choices will not go away on their own. Better to confront them in all their reality from the very first.

Following this are separate chapters on what might be called the building blocks of strength, or for those who have become lost in weakness, the steps on "the way back" to self-confidence and strength. The first of these is love, the essential ground of involvement that is the solid basis upon which all strength—both coping and transcendent—will one day stand. After love, the most basic strength that the child must acquire is responsibility, and then discipline. Next comes work, a crucial stage that has been sadly misrepresented and misunderstood in our society. The final chapters of this section identify the highest kinds of strength known to man: play and faith. These, too, are strengths that have been so caricatured, forgotten, or corrupted in our society that only a long, slow approach and a lot of clarifying discussion will serve to restore these activities and attitudes to their rightful place in the repertoire of human possibility.

The book concludes with a chapter that poses the question, why have children? One might think this should precede the rest, for why bother reading on if you haven't already decided to have a child or if you don't already have one or two or more. And yet, I firmly believe that this question cannot be realistically or deeply answered without an awareness of the effort, the choices, the love and worth—themes that run throughout the book—involved in raising children. In a way, it is a question that parents never stop answering, even if it takes the form later: what am I going to do now that I have children? or why the hell did I have them? In the end, it may be a question that only the parent and child *together* can fully answer.

CHAPTER 2

Choices

I almost caught a butterfly
I really truly did
I had it in my hand
But it got away
        Said the little kid

I almost caught that pass today
We would have won the game
I had it
And I dropped it
        Said the youth with shame

I almost closed that deal today
I had it in my hand
I had it and I lost it
        Said the angry man

Today I caught a butterfly
I held it in my hand
Such a lovely butterfly
I let it fly away
        This was a very old man

                  Jeanne Dean

Whether we admit it or not—and too often we flee responsibility in excuses and rationalizations—we sculpt out the content of our lives in the hard granite of daily choices. Some choices are easy to make: what kind of candy to buy, what to make for dinner, what model car to buy, and so on. Others are harder: what to major in in college, how to allocate income to accommodate needs and wishes, when and whom to marry, and so forth.

In some situations a wrong choice, or *any* choice, may bring pain and suffering. Take the case of an adult with three young children who is considering marriage to a partner who clearly does not get along with the children, and whom the children do not especially care for. What is this person to do? To take the marital plunge might be courting disaster and domestic unrest; to avoid it might result in personal loneliness for the adult and parental absence for the children. This case exemplifies whole ranges of mutual decisions which people in tandem must arrive at—choices about jobs, places to live, lifestyles, and so forth: hard choices, but all of them necessary.

There is yet another kind of choice, very influential in our lives, yet somewhat unconscious because we do not wish to admit to ourselves and others that our behavior, words, and thoughts are chosen. Like ostriches we hope to escape responsibility for patterns of unconscious choice by burying our heads and pretending we didn't make them. "It just happened to me," we think (and lead others to think). "There is nothing I can do about it." Not surprisingly, the first step in counseling people who have painted themselves into painful corners with such choices is to get them to see, to understand, and, above all, *to take responsibility for,* what they have chosen in their lives.

As a rule of thumb, choices about varieties of pleasure are the easiest and the most consciously arrived at. On the other hand, choices that aim at relieving pain, particularly intense psychological pain, are the most desperate, least rational, and often least conscious.[1] These latter choices are usually those which, in the short run, make us feel better but often *at our own expense or at the expense of someone else.*

A word about psychological pain. It is usually brought on by our own behavior—even external crises over which we have little or no control can be intensified by our behavior. Psychological suffering results from the inability to maintain satisfying relationships with people (love) or to develop an abiding feeling of confidence (worth) through what we do. The absence of love brings on loneliness; the absence of worth creates feelings of inadequacy. The ensuing pain is the psyche's way of informing us of our deprivation. The suffering can sometimes become so intense that it will cause the person to concentrate on relieving the symptoms (e.g., migraines, hypertension, depression, guilt, etc.) rather than effecting changes in the basic behavior that has brought on the loneliness or inadequacy in the first place.

Before the discussion becomes too general, however, I shall ground it in a specific example. Let's take the case of Joseph, age thirteen, a student in the eighth grade of a large junior high school in a major city—he is really a composite of many young people I have worked with. His folks have just announced to him they are separating, possibly with the intention of seeking a divorce. At the same time he has received his grades at school, and the "F" in math has resulted in his being thrown off the football team. In a word, the boy has sustained a bitter defeat in the two dimensions of a satisfying life: love and worth. Regarding the separation, Joseph feels an added element of pain because he has heard his parents arguing about him, thus leading him to imagine, wrongly, that he is responsible for the family's breakup.

The situation is clearly not a pleasant one and nobody could truthfully claim that Joseph's choices and decisions

[1] See William Glasser, *Positive Addiction* (New York: Harper & Row, 1976), Chapter One.

would lead him to instant relief and lasting pleasure. But life presents people, young and old, with situations like this (many much worse), and the task of the human being is to meet and transcend them. For Joseph, distraught, guilty, disappointed, angry, the best choice may indeed not appear to be the easiest. The easiest choice is to give up, and Joseph chose this easy way. He simply capitulated before the apparently superior forces of pain and said, in effect: "Okay, then, I don't need them [his parents] anyhow; to hell with school and football. That's for the squares!"

In making such a statement, did Joseph consciously choose to renounce the human quest for love and worth? Probably not, but the fact remains that it launched him on just such a course. The response Joseph made probably felt good . . . for a while. It relieved unbearable pain, like novocain in the dentist's chair, but like novocain, it did nothing to change the pain-causing situation. It would wear off in time.

Joseph's choice was made from a position of pain and of weakness. He had no reserves to draw upon in order to give a positive answer to the challenge life had thrown at him. If, however, his stance had been anchored in strength, he might have tolerated the pain and come to grips with a tough situation. He might have devised a plan, for instance, that would allocate more time for study (possibly with a tutor) and defer his desire for immediate gratification in football. As for his difficult home situation, Joseph might have opted to work at the one thing he did have some control over—his relationship with each parent.

In sum, if Joseph had been different from other American children his age, if he had had the kind of strength that (in this sort of sticky fix) translates into faith in his ability to do what is best, he would have gained much valuable experience and growth which would have stood him in good stead later on. Indeed, just as the choices of weakness are self-perpetuating, so taking the harder, wiser path has the added benefit of reinforcing one's personal sense of will and responsibility and of bolstering the very arsenal of strength needed in order to follow through on the course one has chosen.

But for Joseph to have made this stronger choice, it would have had to be *a conscious one,* arrived at with intelligence, reflection and consultation; he would have needed a wider sense of the *options* open to him. Lack of successful previous experience with resourceful options and wise choices could seriously reduce the likelihood of Joseph's knowing what to do, or even if he knew what to do, of having the self-confidence to do it. Just as importantly, the lack of such examples from his parents' behavior impoverished their son's ability to cope and transcend. When we are confronted by stress and our spectrum of viable alternatives is narrow and uncreative, it is not surprising that we try first to relieve the pain. Certainly Joseph did so by abandoning the search for love and worth altogether. The fact that he took the easy, ultimately more passive and destructive path is hardly unpredictable if we take a look at the boy's past.

Like many American children, Joseph was born into a home where the parents had concluded that their main obligation to their son was to provide for his material welfare, where communication consisted mostly of directions, greetings, and banalities, and where time spent together between parents and child was largely limited to the TV room or to transportation to and from school, church, and playground.

As a result, from the beginning Joseph learned to conceive love in terms of passivity, material giving, and superficial communication. Young people rarely need the lectures and exhortations of their parents; almost always they emulate the *adult* behavior which they see. Thus, in Joseph's case, the boy might ape his father's quick anger at inconveniences or lack of immediate gratification, or his mother's manipulativeness and sulkiness when she doesn't get her way.

The boy is used to getting what he wants, or being yelled at, but not spoken to. His pleasure in his home revolves around the television set and its promised "fast, fast, fast relief." Joseph's mechanisms for coping are brittle and weak. They work only so long as life throws nothing unexpected, nothing deeply frustrating, nothing complicated and long-term his way. When such situations arise, as they have now in the boy's fourteenth year, he cannot bear the pain of loneliness and failure, so he simply elects the All-American path for frustrated youngters: to quit.

What does it mean to quit? Obviously problems don't go away because someone refuses to face them. Problems are not living, intelligent opponents across a chess table who somehow chalk up a point in their favor and then move on. Problems are the self- and life-created obstacles and complexities of one's own existence in society. In this sense, they are like errors made while weaving a tapestry: they never go away; sooner or later you *have* to resolve them. Thus, for Joseph, as for all of us, quitting means avoiding, and avoiding means delaying . . . simply, stubbornly, consciously or unconsciously delaying the time when he will finally *have* to face reality.

As William Glasser wrote in *Positive Addiction,* one of the most unfortunate lessons any child learns in his infancy or youth is to give up.[2] When a child is upset, in pain or difficulty, a parent is well advised to do everything possible to encourage him to hang on somehow so that he doesn't learn to make the simple, but disastrous, choice that Joseph made: "to hell with it." We see examples of this behavior all around us. It is a common pattern, and a formidably hard one to break. So, again, try hard to teach your children not to give up, for if they can internalize the commitment to working in pain, they have learned a very valuable lesson.

I have learned in years of therapy with young people and adults that it is a mistake to get bogged down in the client's "problems." Take Joseph, for example. The lad has many problems—his poor grades, his inability to get along with his

[2] Ibid., pp. 7–11.

folks, not making the team, etc.—which will magnetize his attention and that of the therapist or counselor, if the latter allows himself to get sucked into the never-ending discussion of them. Joseph's *real* problem is deeper than the boy realizes: it is the absence of coping strength. The seeming problems which bedevil him are not so much genuine, tangible obstacles in their own right as they are the direct and indirect results of Joseph's inability and unwillingness to cope. He has resigned under moderately heavy fire, as it were, and that was when his problems began.

Growth and maturity are not easy, and they cannot be made easy or bypassed. The challenge of growth lies in handling the pain of stress. If you reflect about it for just a moment, you'll realize that a child's life entails innumerable daily encounters with discomfort, strain, change, conflict, adaptation. The stresses range from overwhelming to mundane: taking criticism, putting up with an exasperating sibling or parent, suffering physical injury, breaking a toy, adjusting to the loss of a loved one or the death of a pet, being barred from a team because of being too short or too slight, having to get up early, losing a job or not getting one, having no money, being discriminated against because of race or ethnic background, enduring a physical handicap, waking up to a rainy Saturday, etc. ad infinitum.

All of these situations contain the seeds of possible problems because all of them confront the child with the choice of whether or not he will cope or quit. Initially, coping may mean nothing more than learning to live with stress while realizing that not all problems are amenable to ready-made solutions. The pain of irresolution, disappointment, loss, or failure cannot be bypassed or quickly resolved; it must be borne. A gymnast sprains her ankle and cannot finish the season with her team. Is she bitter, angry, moody, impossible to live with? Does she lose interest in everything and everyone in her world? Or does she accept the injury for what it is and cheerfully, or at least resolutely, go about doing the best she can in a physically and psychologically painful situation?

Making the best of a bad moment, finding a way out, creating good out of bad—this is the next step in a coping that goes beyond stoic toleration. To transcend disappointment and difficulty a child needs imagination and creativity. Creativity, especially. A creative child feels no less upset or uncomfortable in the presence of stress than does a weak child, *but he reacts differently to the same negative stimulus.* Instead of fleeing or avoiding it, he comes to grips with it.

Take the child whose family moves into a new neighborhood. The youngster is suddenly dropped into a new school and social environment. This is a tremendous and very common burden on children in our society. A child who has already scored some successes in creative coping will face the new challenge with confidence that he can make friends and make his way in the new world. That confidence is strength as surely as muscles and intelligence are, and far more surely than wealth or status.

The role of the parent is not to shield the child from contact with stress—parents couldn't do so if they tried, but in trying they can foster illusions in the youngster's mind. Rather, the role of the parent is to remind the child that stress is inevitable, and that no matter how painful or overwhelming it seems, the child retains the ability to make choices, for better or for worse. Often it will prove difficult to convince an unhappy youngster that he possesses the possibility of autonomy and choice. The child will want to be told, on the contrary, that life has been cruel and mean, and that there is nothing he can do about it. He will want Mom or Dad to intervene and solve the problem. The parents must gently remind the child that there is *always* something he can do about it, even if the only good choice open to the youngster is to tolerate pain for a while. Fostering a mental attitude of choice-consciousness is thus absolutely essential if the young person is to develop confidence in his ability to live responsibly.

Children who are conscious of their ability to choose have already gained a big advantage over those who take refuge from autonomy and responsibility in excuses, parental rescue, quitting, or avoidance. What is important to keep in mind, however, is that weak children who opt out and quit have still *chosen* to do so—although it may be damnably hard to convince them of that. A defensive characteristic of weakness is that it will not admit to its identity; indeed, weakness often parades as strength and gives the child the illusion of autonomy and success. Precisely because the choices of weakness are so numerous and varied in our society, it is important to inspect and analyze some of the more common among them in order to remind all of us what happens when a young person is unable to cope.

Nothing gives a weak child a more believable illusion of strength than acting out. "Acting out" is a psychological term which applies to a person who tries to solve an internal or personal problem or conflict through difficult or upsetting social behavior. For a child, acting out usually entails fighting, tantrums, excessive teasing, making loud noises, and so forth. It is a despairing and often successful bid for attention. For an infant, acting out may amount to a fit of temper or a gush of tears and abuse of self or others. It's basically another way of saying, "I am going to yell, scream, and carry on until someone pays attention to me or until what's bothering me stops."

Another example concerns a teen-age girl who wants to hitchhike across country with a girlfriend. The mother says, "No, you might get hurt or killed," and the daughter, used to getting her own way, replies by acting out, "Damn it, I want to go, and by God that's what I'm going to do. To hell with you and your silly ideas. Nobody will harm me. I'm leaving."

Here we see the all-too-familiar unconcerned arbitrariness of a frustrated teen-ager in America. In this instance the girl's mother has not established over the years any sort of meaningful communication with her child that would ensure a calm discussion of opposing viewpoints based on mutual respect. Many young people in our society are materially indulged and spoiled, but they often retain sufficiently loving and respectful relationships with their parents that they will hesitate a long time before choosing to act out, particularly in a way that would hurt their folks. In other words, *if some base of initial caring exists, a lot of stress and even a certain amount of selfishness and irresponsibility can be tolerated without despairing of the child's strength for coping.*

There are, unfortunately, many ways to act out. Talking back to adults, drags down Main Street in souped-up cars, fighting in the schoolyard, and doing "wheelies" on a motorcycle in the parking lot during class time are examples of teenage acting out. So is striking another child, fighting with a brother or sister, torturing the family pet, and other violent, disruptive, or rude behavior.

The important point is this: to qualify as worrisome, acting out must be chronic and severe. We all get angry once in a while, we all occasionally take out our anger on the people close to us. Acting out becomes serious only when over a period of time it clearly represents a child's chosen reaction to events, conflicts, or stress which he cannot handle in any other way—when it becomes a pattern of the child's behavior.

So take note of your child's obstreperous behavior. Is it frequent? Does it follow specific kinds of upset or stress? Is it aimed at one recurrent situation or person? Does the choice of behavior (or object) appear to have some connection with a deeper, underlying conflict? Does the momentary excitement and attention of the acting-out behavior clearly afford the child a measure of relief from some other pain? From a young person's perspective, after all, the thrill of stealing a car and going for a joyride is better than living quietly with the constant, dull aching pain of failure, overwhelming stress, or criticism.

The acting out is *chosen behavior,* though the child may not realize or accept this truth. And it may work momentarily, but only at the price of creating greater pain in the long run. Acting out, if it becomes the child's central answer to all challenges and strains, will very likely land him in jail before he is thirty. "It can't happen here," you say, but it can and does happen to one out of every six male children (i.e., they will be referred to juvenile court before they are eighteen—and that is only the beginning).

As common as acting out is in our society, it isn't the only recourse available to a young person who lacks the strength, creativity, or confidence to cope. Depression (or moodiness or sullenness—it has different names) is a frequently chosen alternative. In this condition the child is dejected, anxious, tense, passive, and melancholy because he is internalizing his bad feelings (i.e., turning them onto himself) rather than inflicting them on others by acting out.

Why would a child choose to be moody or depressed rather than act out? Well, for one thing, he may already have tried acting-out behavior and found the price too great in terms of pain. Perhaps the child has been fired from a job or kicked out of school for irresponsible and disruptive behavior. Usually we choose to act out in situations where we can get away with it, where we can inflict pain, disruption, and shock without reaping the consequences—hence, taking out anger on the dog, or beating a smaller classmate, threatening a much younger sibling, or being mean to a permissive and senile grandmother. Only the hard-core delinquent will persevere in acting out when his violent behavior brings him into punitive contact with authority.

Children learn much of this behavior from patterns in their parents' lives. If a father is cruel to his family because he can't stand his boss, but if he is friendly, even sycophantic, when the boss comes to the house, the child will soon learn that there are occasions when being a bully and a boor are apparently acceptable and relieving, and other occasions when servility is in order.

Depression is a more subtle choice of negative behavior

than acting out. It fools the outside world into serving your weakness much more successfully than does overtly antisocial behavior. Depression, like illness or boredom, asks the implicit question of whoever comes into contact with the child: "Something is wrong, what are *you* going to do for me?" Depression settles around the child's head like a shroud, insulating him from contact with the truth—i.e., that *he has decided* to be introverted, sulky, and passive because it's easier than coming to grips with life's problems and solving them.

The key to the parent's behavior is not to buy the child's version of events and come running sympathetically to his rescue. That is a trap, and ultimately there is no rescue except Operation Bootstrap, whereby the youngster accepts responsibility for his negative decision (to be depressed). If frequent bouts of introversion and moodiness characterize your child's response to stress, it is a sign of weakness. As moving and heartrending as a depressed youngster may be, the parent is ill-advised to try to deal with the dejection per se either by intellectualizing it, or commiserating, or in any way becoming implicated in the symptom creation. Instead, the parent should ask the child what he is doing that is causing him to be so depressed, thus placing the responsibility where it belongs—with the child.

Acting out and moodiness certainly do not exhaust the gamut of negative responses to stress. In our society another classic avoidance of pain and complication is addiction to various mind- and body-altering products. Let's go back to our young friend Joseph. In his acting out, he started hanging around the wrong kind of people—youngsters who have, or appear to have, ready-made answers to life's problems. "How are things goin', Joe? Not so good? Well, then, try a few of these," and he offers the boy some dope, or pills, or acid, or maybe cocaine or heroin. Joseph may ask why, but once he's taken the magical potion, he knows why: his problems are (or seem to be) over. In place of apathy, anxiety, guilt, frustration, he feels animated, talkative, euphoric, mellow—in a word, free.

It is only a matter of time before he will establish a connection in his mind between the bad feelings he experiences because of his problems and the rush of immediate sensual/emotional gratification he derives from the drug. If he is a weak child, with few resources of his own to fall back on, the temptation of the drug's easy-way-out becomes irresistible.

Social disruptiveness and introversion give little joy. But frequent use of drugs, or alcohol, or overeating give great pleasure. This simple fact makes it *all the more difficult to wean the young person away from this kind of self-weakening behavior*. He has found a seemingly sturdy crutch, a "successful" alternative to confronting reality, which permits him to continue the ineffectual life he has chosen. More than likely, too, he has become involved in a supportive subculture which reinforces his decision to give up.

Virtually the same things can be said for alcohol, except that its effects on a person's brain, liver, nervous system, and digestive tract are more immediately harmful than many drugs are. Alcohol is particularly tempting to young people because their elders' use of it is so visible. Being legal, alcohol is also available without the hassle and risk of drugs. Even if the parents are cautious, selective users of alcohol, the child—in his pain—may not discriminate or distinguish his parents' use from his own growing dependency.

Addictive or escapist behavior of all kinds—from drugs to alcohol to gambling to overeating—is very much learned behavior. The media, especially television, extol escapism and surrender. Madison Avenue regularly creates "needs" and then palms off products designed to "meet" those "needs." From cradle to grave, Americans are acculturated to expect fabricated answers and products for every exigency and problem of life. Drugs are taken for emotional tranquility, to sleep, for sexual potency, for sore throats, to stay awake, to avoid smoking, to curb appetite, to prevent pregnancy, to relieve pains and aches of all sorts, to calm the tense and to energize the apathetic—in short, pills are employed in all those areas of life where hard work, discipline, will power, patience, intelligence, love, and communication were once necessary.

Our dependency upon drugs is now so great that pediatricians are reporting increasing numbers of parents who administer tranquilizers and stimulants to infants! Last year, for example, in an upper-middle-class suburb, a mother took her three-year-old to a doctor. The little boy was fidgety and restless, complained the woman (what three-year-old isn't sometimes?). Could the pediatrician please prescribe Valium? He did . . . for the mother. On another occasion, a worried mother called her pediatrician to report that she couldn't awaken her child from a six-hour sleep. Upon questioning the woman, the doctor learned that she had been giving her son doses of a sedative because "he just wouldn't stop crying."

The point of these two tales is not that parents are becoming cruel and unconcerned, but rather that Americans are increasingly unwilling to tolerate the slightest disturbances—especially when it appears that recourse to drugs (or alcohol) will "cure" them. The irony of administering drugs to children, somehow lost on the parents who do it, is that the habit naturally reinforces a potential drug dependency in the child when he gets older. The same mother who frets that her daughter will get "hooked" on dope or heroin has unwittingly set the stage for this denouement earlier by giving her Valium or Percodan or Sominex.

Parents must remember that much of the behavior that troubles them in their children is just a normal part of development. A toddler who is afraid of the dark, and who cries and carries on, does not need a mild dose of Ritalin; he needs to be allowed to work through the experience of separateness and darkness for himself. Drugs only postpone and complicate the learning experience which any child *must* undergo in growing up. What he needs from his parents is not artificial sedatives or stimulants but rather love, patience, energy, intelligence, support.

What the parents are passing on to their offspring is not just the habit of drug-taking, but of *avoidance*—the false and debilitating notion that all of life's difficulties (or many of them) can somehow be skirted and dodged by external, technological, medical or psychiatric panaceas. If Job had had recourse to the defensive nostrums of our society, he might have suffered less, to be sure . . . but he would never have known God. Okay, so we're not all Jobs. The point is *not* that suffering is good, but that a certain amount of frustration and pain are *inevitable* in life, and you only lessen your own or your child's ability to surmount life's obstacles by attempting to remain insulated from them.

Even if you wanted to, you couldn't. Drugs—like liquor or excuses or deceits or any other avoidance behavior—merely put off the eventual day of reckoning and make its confrontation many times more painful. Ultimately, they are the self-weakening, self-betraying, futile devices of people who live in fear . . . and who therefore fear to live.

We have dwelt in some detail on drugs and alcohol because they are so common to our culture, but there are many other popular types of addictive/avoidance behavior which adults pass on to children. Overeating, of course, is as All-American as apple pie. "Junkfood junkies" are simply this generation's answer to two decades of Madison Avenue hype-sell of every variety of refined, processed, packaged, profitable garbage. Food is a classic compensation for anyone who suffers from feelings of inferiority or loneliness.

Another of the commonest compensations is physical illness. Since as far back as classical Greece, men have known that mind and body, feelings and spirit are interrelated, that an imbalance among them, or a debilitation in one area, can lead to a malfunctioning of the whole. In current medical theory there is an entire category of maladies known as "diseases of civilization," because they seem so closely to accompany the stress, competitiveness, hypertension, anxiety, and criticism of modern society. Ailments like ulcers, migraines, heart disease, diarrhea, backaches, high blood pressure, and many more maladies are now considered as the physical mirrors of emotional and psychological strain.

What does this have to do with our overwhelmed child in search of a way to avoid the stress of reality? The answer is apparent: school infirmaries across the land are plagued with youngsters who complain of everything from headaches to stomachaches to asthma. Not all these physical ailments are illusory, nor are they necessarily the results of emotional distress, but in far more cases than most parents realize, the physical problems—even perhaps the injuries of accident-prone children—may have a decisively psychological dimension.

Like depression, only more so, physical sickness exempts a child from involvement in life. After all, nobody expects much of a person confined to "the sick role." For the parent who thinks his child's illness may be psychosomatic, the crucial questions to ask are these: Is my child usually happy? Does he have sources of love and worth? Is this particular ailment unusual in his healthy history? If the answer to any of these questions is no, then the parent is advised not only to treat the physical illness, of course, but also to scrutinize carefully the possible links it may have with feelings of inadequacy, loneliness, or pressure—in other words, to begin treating the cause, not merely the symptoms.

In some extreme cases, children may elect tragically negative choices. Suicide and attempted suicide are two such examples. According to Dr. Pamela Cantor, chairperson of the American Association of Suicidology, four hundred thousand young people attempt suicide every year, and one out of every two children has thought about it. Over the last ten years, there has been an increase of 200 per cent in the number of attempted suicides by young people.

In other instances, children may choose symptoms that are psychotic (e.g., hallucinations, delusions, paranoia, etc.), or they may simply begin to act "a little crazy." Such children retire completely into a world of fantasy because the reality of family, school, and society seems temporarily overwhelming. By inhabiting a delusion, the child is able to confer love and worth upon himself which he couldn't do in reality. Psychosis is a drastic alternative, however, and occurs infrequently. But to conceive of it, as contemporary psychiatry does, as some sort of "mental illness" that "happens to somebody," instead of as a self-created, self-willed defense against reality prevents the suffering person from coming to grips with himself.

In concluding this discussion of the harmful ways a weak child may select to avoid working through a tough situation, let me underscore again the source of many of these weak choices. *Children learn them from the people closest to them: their parents.* If mothers and fathers are perennially complaining of headaches, it is hardly astonishing if the child learns to get headaches. If a father indulges in excessive displays of rage and anger, if he readily hides behind excuses and rationalizations, if he avoids difficult discussions or considers it unmanly to show love, the child is sure to detect these traits (even if his awareness only hovers in his preconscious), and the chances are good that one day he will emulate this avoidance behavior by taking refuge in deceits, rationalizations, and symptoms. Thus, the important thing for parents to remember is this: *the example you set by your behavior, not your sermons, is your most important contribution to your child's learning process.*

I must confess at this point to having derived small satisfaction from analyzing in such detail the anatomy of weakness and avoidance which has become the backbone of too many American children—for the motivation and purpose of this book are practical, optimistic, hopeful. Nonetheless, in order for qualities such as optimism to be realistic, it seemed essential to look squarely at the unhappy alternatives.

The title of this chapter—CHOICES—is a double-edged sword. As young people regularly choose to give up, evade, retreat, *so may they also choose to stand fast, fight hard, tran-*

scend creatively. This choice, too, is habit-forming, life-effect-
ing. As hope was the last spirit to fly from Pandora's box, in
the wake of all the demons and plagues, so the possibility of
choosing to regain lost strength is the hope which remains
when all the symptoms, copouts, addictions, and avoidances
have been examined.

PART II

The Way Back

CHAPTER 3

Love

Between the dark and the daylight
When the night is beginning to lower,
Comes a pause in the day's occupations,
That is known as the Children's Hour.

Henry Wadsworth Longfellow

A distraught mother called me at my office not long ago. She was very worried about her seven-year-old son, who was seriously hyperactive. She and her husband had already tried a number of therapists and counselors, but apparently to no avail. With some desperation the woman asked me if I would treat her boy. As is my custom in such situations, I asked the woman if she and her husband would first come in and see me by themselves. In my experience it does no good at all to work exclusively with young people, particularly primary-grade children. I insist always on working with the child's environment, which, at very young ages, means the parents.

The woman listened to my explanation and request, and promised to call me back the next day. When she did so, it was to inform me that her husband was neither interested in talking with me about his son nor desirous of participating in the counseling process. She added, "All Jack wants is for you to make Billy normal again." I asked the mother if she herself would at least be willing to come in and speak with me. She hesitated a moment and then dutifully replied that she "kind of" agreed with her husband, and that it was Billy, "not us," who needed treatment. I sadly informed the lady that I could not help her and that I would only be wasting her money to consent to work with Billy alone.

One of the most misleading illusions of our society is that problems of character, personality, and general well-being are somehow isolated snags that can be "cleared up" by a prescription, by testing, or by calling in an expert. I don't know what specifically might have been causing hyperactive symptoms in Billy, but I have never yet worked with a young person—hyperactive, depressed, acting out, psychosomatically ill, etc.—whose problems could not be at least partially resolved by creating a loving relationship between him and his parents. Indeed, in most instances the problems and symptoms have their roots in the absence or distortion of a truly loving relationship in the family.

In the case of Billy, I would even hypothesize that there is a critical relationship between the child's underlying problem and his father's refusal (avoidance behavior) to see me. I sensed fear in that father's refusal even to call me on the telephone, and the fear was probably of my finding out how he was involved in Billy's problem. In my mind, there is a clear link between Jack's eagerness to call in "experts" to "treat" Billy and his own failure to spend significant time with his son.

Billy's predicament and Jack's evasion lead me to the central tenet of this chapter: *the most enduring basis of strength is love.* And by love I do not merely mean something that warms the cockles of your heart. In many years of experience, I have learned (sometimes the hard way) that endearing words, pats, and protestations are only the pretty face of love. They take on real luster and beauty only as they are supported underneath by the sinew, muscle, mind, and heart of love. In all cases, the meaning of love lies in its action and combining power—its "valence," to borrow a term from chemistry.

The demand of love cannot be hedged or temporized. It necessarily and fundamentally means *spending time with your child.* You are either willing to pay the price of time, or you are not; the child knows instantly. No amount of material benificence, not lip service or promises, not good intentions or favors or services rendered, not kisses and hugs, not a superior educational opportunity or material and social advantage—*not anything* will suffice to take the place of loving time spent with a child. In the absence of the latter, the former slowly dissolve into shadows and façades, forms without substance, words and things without actions. Although I shall have more to say in the course of this chapter about love, it finally boils down to one principle: By this your child will know you love him—*that you spend time with him.*

Love is simple, but it is not easy. The great French philosopher Pascal once said of love that it is the one thing that doesn't have to be reinterpreted and explained. From era to era, love simply demonstrates itself as clearly and distinctly as the ring of Steuben crystal.

The predisposition toward love is natural to man; but the expression of love, the willingness to spend time, the wisdom of how to spend it, are all learned behavior. Indeed I would hope and assume that the reader of this book—whether a counselor, teacher, friend, or parent—is basically willing to spend time with young people. If not in the habit of doing so already, you would be well-advised from the start to realize that to create the pattern is not altogether painless. It requires interrupting what you are doing in your adult life, or scheduling special time, or sometimes reorienting your plans, for the sake of a nine-year-old.

Many times it will be very easy to postpone or cancel or compromise on the quality and quantity of this time, and often it will seem useless to you in terms of immediate tangible benefits. But you will be making a grave mistake if you give in to such stimuli and self-centered second thoughts. The child needs to know you love; he needs to interact with you; he needs the strength that such interaction and such a dependable, consistent, enduring relationship offers. More than anything else, this relationship will provide the child (and the adult, too, for that matter) with a granite base of strength upon which to build his life.

I would offer my own experiences as an illustration of what I am saying. My parents have both been dead for many years. While they lived, they were extremely involved with civic and social concerns. They were both very intelligent and impressive people. But as I look back, I remember little of what they said, and even their many good works now seem far away and long ago, products of another era.

What remains with me, however, is the legacy of their time spent with me. When I was very little, my father read to me regularly—Dickens, especially, I recall. We made our way through practically every volume. And together we listened to Gilbert and Sullivan. We not only listened to the records, we read the librettos and went to the productions when they came to town. My mother often took me with her on her rounds of charity. And when I say "took me with her," I don't mean as tag-along baggage. She took the time and interest to show me what she was doing, to help me to participate, and from these moments of interaction we grew close.

My parents, in other words, showed their love for me by giving me liberally of their time, by integrating me into their lives. I learned values and faith, not so much from their words, but from their actions; and those values and that faith have remained the mainspring of my strength for coping.

In this chapter, then, rather than discourse at length about the "wondrous beauty of love," I will try to take a hard, practical look at the subject. Exploring further the theme of time, we shall see that essentially there are two ways to best fill it: shared activity toward a common goal, and talking. Dealing with activity first, we will establish some pragmatic criteria—

effort, value, play, self-discipline, being alone with a child—
which go into selecting and structuring the time. Obviously
these elements are not intended to be present all at the same
time; but if, in various kinds of activity you touch all these
bases, your love for your child will be effective. Then in talking about talking, I will outline some of the do's and don'ts of
making conversation with young people.

One final point to keep in mind as you read on: there are no
hard-and-fast rules. In the first and last analysis, spending loving, strength-building time with a young person is very much
an improvisational, open-minded, unpredictable proposition
requiring spontaneity, resourcefulness, patience, intelligence,
sacrifice, and perseverance. It is a lot harder than reading (or,
for that matter, writing) this book.

I have on several different occasions in this book noted that
the value of words, especially in the form of lip service, is
drastically inflated these days. This is true even of the time you
spend with a child. As a rule of thumb, then, *it is best, in the
beginning especially, to fill the moments spent with a young
person by doing something, performing some activity in which
you can both lose yourselves and find each other.* In other
words, don't go running off to your daughter, age seven, and
engage her in a "serious conversation." You'll probably bore
or puzzle her, fluster yourself, and impress both of you with
the artificiality of the effort.

Indeed, one of the truly remarkable things about activity is
the way it permits and animates communication, certainly an
essential component of a loving relationship. A father of a
difficult seventeen-year-old son might encounter heavy going if
he squares off with the boy in a Dutch-uncle discussion, but he
would soon discover that the level of mutual understanding
(not to mention simple pleasure) could be raised if he and his
son spend a few evenings together searching the car lots for a
new family automobile or painting a room or hanging pictures. The point here is an important one: the father is *not*

buying the boy a car, he is doing what had to be done anyway (i.e., purchase a new family automobile), and he is doing it with his son, asking the boy's advice, and perhaps taking it.

Another way of putting it is that time with a young person is best spent when it centers around some meaningful *act*ivity. I underscore the first syllable of the word because clearly not all time spent with kids has equal value. For example, watching television together, or going to the movies, even though the latter requires a jot more effort (you have to drive somewhere), or going to a place where the only option is to listen to loud music are far from adequate as means of fostering communication and rapport.

While I'm leveling a lance at some of society's sacred cows, let me take on one of the great Brahmin bulls of suburbia. The time spent sitting in a station wagon being transported hither and yon by Mommy also doesn't qualify as *meaningful activity,* even if it does permit a parent and child lots of time together. Driving in city traffic is probably the most infuriating experience since being lectured by a petty bureaucrat; it is not conducive to paying attention to a conversation, nor to patience, nor to tranquility, nor affection. In fact, if Women's Lib has any impact at all, I hope it will be in the area of emancipating the middle-class housewife from the shackles of driving the kids everywhere. Let 'em walk, or ride their bikes, or take the bus, or stay home.

The point is this: *any essentially passive experience, even if done together, doesn't contribute much to the human intercourse from which strength can come.*

In concluding this fulmination against passivity, I want to say a word about loud music, especially of the rock variety. It may sound like I have some old-fogey prejudice against "the new sounds." I do not. What I am criticizing is not the music, but the narrow mode of social interaction which surrounds this country's youth when they hear music.

I remember countless occasions when I went to see my teenage son John at school. Walking down the hall of his dorm was like walking through a recording studio. Behind each door the muffled pulsations and blasts of hard "rock" (or "country") struggled to break out of the tiny confines of the dormitory room. Bracing myself, I would open the door to my son's cell (fruitless to knock, you'd have needed a sandblaster to be heard) and be met by an overwhelming assault on my auditory faculties. It always took a few minutes to adjust, but finally I'd feel free enough from the throb of an enraged eardrum to be able to take a look around the room (no easy task either: a miasma of marijuana hung like smog over the Los Angeles basin).

The same scene always greeted me. Four or five handsome, athletic, intelligent young men lay scattered about like so many throw rugs, hanging over chairs in serpentine coils, not speaking a word. It reminded me of an opium den in Shanghai during the war, or a room in a geriatric hospice in Calcutta. Nor was this scene unusual; it represented much of what many of these boys did together when they weren't sleeping, studying, or in class. It *was* a large share of their social interaction. In discussing my observations with John later, he admitted as much. Many of his mates really didn't know how to talk to each other. They immersed themselves in the decibels as a means of escape—an activity (or passivity) frighteningly similar to their earlier immersion in television.

The music provides a medium of escape for many kids. It is like floating in a dark, warm, deep sea of oblivion. No strength comes out of this experience, no expansion of mind, body, or spirit, no increased capacity for creative coping. Many young people don't even enjoy what they are doing: the vacuous looks on their faces show that. They are simply trying to fill a void, whether of loneliness or worthlessness, but the void remains. Too often they do not even know what they are missing: the exhilarating, energizing interaction which their passivity is excluding them from. By titillating, and finally stunning, a couple of sense faculties with loud music and pot,

these young products of our Media Age are searching for the
love and worth which only strength can give them.

It takes very little to wean young people away from joyless
apathy. (In most cases, they really *want* to be pulled out of the
swamp.) In our family room at home, for instance, without
removing the television and causing an insurrection, I installed
a pool table and fussball game. Very shortly, instead of lying
around like lounge lizards staring dumbly at the tube, the kids
took up the pool cues and fussball rods. Their laughter, conversation, friendly competition, and warmth assured me that
seeds of strength were being sown. (The TV set lost a good
50–60 per cent of its running time in the Ford household.)

After a few weeks, kids congregated in our house as if it
were the local pizza hut—simply because there was something
more to do than watch television. By the way, the stereo in the
playroom got a lot of action, too, though the decibel count was
rather lower than in John's dorm room, but the contrast with
his school was crucial: here the "rock" and "country" served
as facilitating background, not psychological formaldehyde.

Enough of the "what-not-to-do's." Let's take a look at the
positive side. What kind of activity works best in establishing
meaningful, strength-building contact between adult and
child? *The primary criterion of all such activity is that it
require effort.* We have already seen that sitting together idly
absorbed in sound or diffidently ingesting food are not conducive to building strength. Effort implies commonality of purpose; indeed, it is axiomatic that *time spent by two or more
people working together toward a common goal builds
strength.*

This seems self-evident, but the fact is that far too often
people lull themselves into the passive, effortless types of entertainment for which years of TV absorption have prepared
them. You can take a child (or an adult) to a movie and to
McDonald's afterwards, and both of you will perhaps feel
good about it, but feelings are rarely trustworthy judges and

indicators of strength-building unless they are sustained, and profound. As a rule of thumb, particularly in the beginning of any project to draw closer to your child, cast an evaluative, critical eye on the activity in question and judge it with your intelligence as well as the surge of warm feelings it evokes.

Effort, then, is a basic criterion of strength-building activity. However, there are further considerations as well. *Value,* for instance, is critical. Does what you are doing have relevance or long-term significance? Playing a game together like pool or chess is pleasurable and strengthening, but it is less valuable than painting the house together, or repairing the car, weeding (or planting) a vegetable garden, working in a political campaign, performing charitable or church-affiliated activities, etc. Before going on, let me stress that I don't mean to downplay the importance of play. Indeed, I believe it is so important that it warrants an entire chapter (Chapter 7).

Returning to the question of value, I recall, for instance, that the most important activities I shared with my mother, in terms of storing up strength, revolved around her work with the church and the community. When I was very young, of course, it was difficult for me to be and to work with people. I needed my mother's assistance and dependable presence. I leaned on her ability to cope with the challenges presented, and that's just as it should be for a young child. But gradually over time, and with her perseverance, I gained confidence. Not only did I grow much closer to my mother, whose life I now partly shared, but in the process I learned to work with people on my own.

I should add that some of the parent-created patterns I learned as a child didn't have such felicitous consequences. My father was a county judge and worked very long hours, including many holidays. The nightly stints with Dickens aside, I spent very little time with him, certainly less than I wanted. He was not a bad person (on the contrary, he was respected by everyone in our community), but like many American fathers, he sacrificed some of his family life for his work.

In recent years, and especially as I got involved in teaching and then in Reality Therapy, I began to reflect on the effect my father had on me and what I was doing as a father. I saw that some of the difficulties my children were having stemmed from my own choice not to spend meaningful time with them. I have now tried to alter my patterns of behavior toward my children, and the effect has been successful, I hope. But it has not been easy, precisely because the pattern set so long ago with my father persisted. It is an old but important insight of modern psychology that the earlier a lesson is learned in life, the longer it is kept and the harder it is to break. That is why where children are concerned, love *must* be translated from the very first as time spent wisely, unsparingly, and lovingly.

So far I have discussed *effort* and *value* as essential qualities or components of the activity that is so important in building a loving relationship with children (or with anybody, for that matter). A third quality is *play* (see Chapter 7). A fourth is *discipline,* which is a large and vital concept. The term has two fundamental and related meanings for us: on the one hand, discipline teaches a child to obey the rules when he isn't doing so or doesn't want to. This aspect will be treated at length in Chapter 5. On the other hand, discipline, especially when it is preceded by the prefix "self," is *the ability to withstand the pain or discomfort of pushing ahead when you really don't want to.*

The key to lasting, strengthful discipline is to get the child to instill it in himself. This is somewhat harder to do than it seems, because children so easily internalize the aspirations of parents. Even if his conscious commitment appears to be wholehearted, there will always be a hidden niche somewhere in the child's heart which knows the truth and stubbornly fights to be free of the externally imposed discipline and goals. Many of this country's greatest athletes, including some celebrated swimmers and tennis stars, never freely chose to pursue their sport, but offered themselves as living sacrifices upon the Altar of Winning for the sake of satisfying a domineering mother or father. The proof is the joylessness and bitterness with which they play their game, and frequently the alacrity with which they retire from it once the sought-after honors are won.

So the key to discipline is to evoke it from the child rather than impose it upon him. In the beginning this crucial distinction may need to be temporarily waived. Initially the child will lean on the adult's confidence and imposed discipline simply because he doesn't know what it is to pursue something with determination and sacrifice. The parent's job is first to make known to his son or daughter that many, indeed most, meaningful activities require a kind of resolve, self-control, and commitment called discipline. Secondly, he offers the child the opportunity to pursue some such activity in a systematic fashion. Most likely the child will already have some preferences and interests of his own which lean clearly in one or two directions.

As the child's interests and talents begin to define themselves clearly, the parent can then specify a program of development for his child in the chosen activity. At this point, and not before, he asks from his son or daughter a commitment—say four months of lessons, practice, discipline—to pursue the activity, even if the going gets rough. Once embarked upon the project, the parent's job is to be *supportive* and *receptive,* not active and interventionary. He must communicate to the child not only interest and sympathy, but also firmness about the commitment and willingness to oblige the child to make good on the agreement.

Firmness may prove difficult for the parent to show—it takes energy, patience, courage "to stay on a kid's case" (as my daughter Terry put it)—but it is essential. To do less, to relent and let the child renege on the commitment, would be to reinforce a giving-up behavior pattern, and would give the child an altogether unrealistic notion of what is required in life in

order to perform anything well enough to derive lasting satisfaction, self-confidence, and strength from it.

Through it all, the adult should at no time permit himself to
transfer his own aspirations and feelings about the activity (or
about winning and succeeding) to the child. The best the adult
can do, at this point, as in the past, is to continue to set his
own example of self-discipline. I have been a daily jogger for
over twelve years, but I have never cajoled or obliged my children to run. Yet, as of this writing, five of my eight children
do some kind of regular daily strenuous physical exercise (two
of them are joggers).

A final criterion for activity on which to found love and
strength is that at times the adult and the child do it *alone,* by
themselves. Particularly in large families, parents have a tendency to do things *en famille*—and this is fine and important.
But there should be some daily time set apart, even if only *five
minutes,* when each parent gets together with each child
separately. Strength-building is not a once-a-week shot; the
amount of time spent is less important than the regularity and
quality of it. Usually the daily five minutes will be pleasurable;
it will serve as a dependable "letting-go" break in the child's
(and the adult's) day.

For instance, I might help my nine-year-old Luke clean his
room while we chat about the day's occupations, or I might
play a game or two of backgammon with Thomas, my twelve-
year-old, or get a short lesson on the latest "rock" or "country"
classic from my fifteen-year-old, Joseph. I used to give each of
my three daughters a hug and kiss when I came home from
work, followed by a short chat about the events of the day.
Now that they are no longer living at home, I try to stay in
close touch with them by telephone and letters.

Did you ever try to *make* conversation with a child?
"Where'd you go?"   "Nowhere."
"What'd you do?"   "Nothin'."

"What'd you learn in school today?" "I dunno."

Not altogether easy, is it? It's kind of like singing a round: both parties say words, but nothing is transmitted. Yet conversation, the exchange of meaningful communication, is the second key way to spend loving time with a young person. If most conversation is difficult and close-ended, it is because the child knows damn well your questions are perfunctory make-talk ("Did you have a nice time in Sunday School, dear?"), or they are anchored in incriminating suspicion ("What were you *doing* with those boys down at the dock anyway?"), or they touch on topics of zero-degree interest to the child ("Do you think Warren Burger was a good choice for Chief Justice of the Supreme Court?").

So how do you talk to young people? Fair question, but let's approach it by asking first, *When* do you talk to young people? As I look back upon my own life, the most important, lasting conversations I had with my parents, and later with my children, were at the dinner table. You may remember there was a time in this country's past when the dinner hour was sacred because it was the principal occasion in the day when a family could be together.

But times have changed, and the uncontested triumph of the fast-food chains bear ugly witness to the disintegration of the dining habits and values of the world of our fathers. Eating together is rarely an experience of closeness, energy, humor, and sharing these days. Instead, family members usually eat separately. And if they should happen to eat in the same room, the experience is usually rushed, silent, and probably focused on the television set. In other words, just because you cajole your family into sitting down to a meal together, it is not necessarily the experience of family togetherness you had hoped and expected it to be. The occasion has to be cultivated and nurtured into a full-blown habit, and even then it is only a base, a chance, a launching pad upon which a lot of effort at conversation, intimacy, humor, and care may perhaps build strength in the participants.

There are of course other times for conversation than the evening meal; in fact, no time should be automatically excluded—even when adult friends drop in. In our family, for example, the mutual sharing of certain of our adult friends is a very important locus of interaction. But if the habit of conversation has eluded you and your family, perhaps the best place to begin a campaign to restore it is at the dinner table.

Okay, so now you're seated around it, what do you say? Of the three principles to keep in mind about conversation with children, the first is to discuss something of common interest. This may appear obvious, but it's easy to lose sight of. If you're at a party and you get caught up in a group of surgeons talking about bilateral salpingo-oophorectomies, you don't force yourself to be interested, you simply leave and try elsewhere. Similarly, with kids, you shouldn't just try to draw them into *your* conversation; the effort will be artificial and probably unsuccessful. But this doesn't mean you have to talk about banalities with children either. The "common" in "common interest" stems from commonality, not commonness. It's not necessary to talk down to young people. Some "sure bets" as to evocative subject matter: recent and distant experiences which the family had together (vacations, jokes, relatives, previous homes, etc.); close friends of the family; planning or discussing an upcoming event, etc.

In the last analysis, however, it's safe to predict that most extended, absorbing discussions with young people will revolve around some aspect of the world they live in. At this point *the commonality of interest really depends upon the adult's willingness and ability to care about, and to some extent share, the world of the child.* This is hard to do; the ability, if it's not God-given, must be cultivated painstakingly and with a fair degree of self-sacrifice. You can't fake it; the child will sense your boredom in an instant. The best advice I can give is to trod gently in this area; don't plunge into a full-dress discussion of their world unless or until you can generate sincere enthusiasm, relevance, concern for an extended period of time.

A second principle to observe when conversing with children is to remain *noncritical*. Learn to accept the expression of a thought even if it's clear to you the thought is wrong or silly. And make sure everyone else at the table stays open. I remember when my teen-age daughter Mary Ellen grew so uncritically enamored by the study of world history that she came to the dinner table each night espousing a different cause. This worked well enough if the hero or movement being apotheosized were Woodrow Wilson or the League of Women Voters; but we had some lessons in patience and tolerance, I'll tell you, when M.E. thought that "the Nazi Third Reich was getting a raw deal" or the tsarist autocracy in Russia "wasn't so bad." If I had replied to my daughter's thoughtless opinions, with sarcasm or outrage, or if I had permitted the other children at the table to do so, a fight or a pouting session would have ensued. By staying noncritical, however—even in the face of provocative words—and by asking questions unemotionally ("What are your reasons for thinking that, Mary Ellen?"), we were able to enjoy some stimulating and thoughtful discussions. Now, many years later, Mary Ellen has changed her views about history, but the examples of forbearance and noncritical discussion continue to affect my daughter's verbal behavior.

The third principle is to make skillful use of the *question*. A good friend of mine is a former correspondent for *Time* magazine. When he dines with us, I notice how attentive and talkative our children are because he knows how to ask questions that elicit not just answers, but responses.

In discussing the art of the question with him, I came up with three basic types of interrogation which elicit answers and evoke responses. The first sort of question is one that admits of many answers: "Who are some of the characters in *Tom Sawyer* that you remember best?" "It's Saturday, kids. What can we do tonight?" "What are your favorite memories of last summer?"

Second, questions seeking opinion work wonders, but only if they are sincere—that is, if the questioner really wants to hear the answer and is willing to be affected by it. You don't have to agree with the opinion expressed—indeed, you may disagree with it—but you do have to want to hear it.

Third, ask questions that demand some *thought* and *creativity:* "How would you have ended this story?" "What character (or scene) did that film require to make it more interesting (believable, profound, humorous, etc.)?" A helpful hint here: it is oftentimes a good idea to *personalize* a situation or role-play a part. I remember a long and lively discussion among my children and some of their friends after we came back from seeing the film *Waterloo.* The personalized question, "How would you have fought the battle if you were Napoleon," quickly gave way to four or five kids playing the parts of Wellington, Napoleon, Blücher, Ney, etc.

Since that not-to-be-forgotten night when I was ten years old and my father first took a volume of Dickens (*Oliver Twist*) from the shelf and read to me thirty minutes before lights out, I have felt that reading to a child is one of the best sources of conversation (and sharing) available. It has the wonderful added advantage of rescuing books from the awe and ignorance with which they are regarded by most children. I know of many cases where young people who hated reading in school and were poor at it developed an interest, even a joy, in reading after their parents had shared *The Wizard of Oz* (or whatever) with them. In selecting books, you might let the child go to the library with you to pick out what he likes—and if he doesn't know what he likes, give him the plot summaries of four or five books and see which one animates him most.

I hope that throughout the sometimes lengthy side journeys of this chapter, the reader has not forgotten the title and subject matter which moves the discussion forward: love. We have seen that love is more than embraces and endearments. It is best expressed toward a young person by the time you spend with him or her in a variety of meaningful, occasionally structured ways. For a young person who has little strength to begin with, or who has lost the strength he had—like our friend Joseph from Chapter 1—the beginning of the road to developing or rebuilding strength lies in the love relationship he shares with the key people in his life, mainly his parents. Their love for him will include affection and assurance, of course, but it will mainly consist of time.

Love is not really enough, however, even though it is fundamental and primary. The following chapters in this book will examine further ways of building strength in a child, but keep in mind that what we build stands always on the base of love.

CHAPTER 4

Responsibility

No man is an island, entire of itself; every man is a piece of the continent, a part of the main . . . any man's death diminishes me, because I am involved in mankind; and therefore never send to know for whom the bell tolls; it tolls for thee.

John Donne

After negative choices have been examined and abandoned, after the basis of loving interaction in a matrix of time spent with your child is established, you are ready to forge ahead with plans, actions, patterns of behavior which will integrate the child into the larger world of which he is a part. In effect, responsibility is the capacity for making positive choices and patterns of choices in society which introduce the young person to some of the strengths of maturity: self-confidence, self-reliance, survival, planning, commitment, execution of intention, and so forth. Responsibility is the first step toward the outside.

But, like charity, responsibility begins in the home. It also begins at the beginning, from the moment the baby comes home from the hospital. One of the very first lessons you can teach a child is *to take care of himself for short periods of time.* For example, parents often come to me saying they have "a very good baby," but every time they put him down he starts to cry until they pick him up again. This is cute for a while, but soon the fun wears off. "What should we do now, Mr. Ford?"

Well, you can teach him his first lesson in responsibility. You can play with your baby a reasonable amount of time, make sure that he is fed, cleaned, bedded down and loved, then say to him, even when he's a week old (Who knows if he understands?), "Son, now take care of yourself for a while." Put him down, close several doors between you and him, and in a short time he will learn to take care of himself for a reasonable period—maybe two or three hours.

The first month of a child's life is the crucial time for him to begin to learn the responsibility that comes from self-reliance. If, from the very start, you make it clear that sometimes he will have to be alone, he'll start to learn to do whatever activities amuse him by himself (gurgle, play with his hands or feet, sleep, etc.). At first he may cry, but there are many kinds of infant cries—you will learn to distinguish them. If the cry is intoned like a wail the moment you close the door—the "come-play-with-me-I'm-bored" cry—then firmly ignore it. If, after a while of being by himself the cry begins to signify "I've-reached-my-limits," then you can go to him with pride and gratitude.

A child who has learned, by the time he reaches school age, to be patient and take care of himself for limited periods of time, is going to be a stronger child than one who has not. This lesson won't be learned by pampering an infant throughout the first five years. Nor will it suddenly be discovered, as some parents mistakenly expect, the moment he enters school. A teacher, even a good one, can't easily derail a child from the track of dependency that his parents have unwittingly put him on in the first five years of life.

I realize that giving responsibility lessons to week-old babies will startle and scandalize a good many American parents. It goes against the sacred tradition in this country of babying the hell out of the infant until he reaches high school age, then suddenly cracking down on the child's freedom and laying a heavy mantle of expectations and accountability on him. My own inclination for teaching freedom and responsibility to young people, runs in a different direction—to instruct a child in the ways of freedom and responsibility from the dawn of his life, and, as he approaches midmorning and noon, increase the range of both.

What is responsibility at bottom? For a young infant, it's realizing his separateness from his parents, especially the mother. It's accepting his individuality and independence, and living with them. As he grows older, it means assuming accountability, the burden of carrying one's own life—no easy matter, by the way, considering how many Americans, young and old, studiously avoid this burden as if it were an evil spirit. But responsibility need not be a cross—even though there are moments in life when it feels like one. The fact is, the experience of genuine responsibility is exhilarating. It is exhilarating precisely because responsibility implies freedom—without freedom, there is no accountability—and in learning to deal wisely with freedom, the young person is experiencing the essence of human life.

Turning from the abstract to the more concrete, *responsibility is the ability of a person to fulfill his needs for love and worth.*[1] If these needs are not met, the child or adult suffers; if the absence of love and worth is extensive enough, he feels real pain. This pain, be it physical or psychological, is not without purpose, however, for it warns the one experiencing it that he is doing something harmful to himself. Unlike the pain of accidentally putting your finger on a hot stove, though, *the ache of the unfulfilled needs of love and worth does not necessarily reveal what to do to stop it.*

This is a particularly important insight to keep in mind when you are dealing with children, because their first instinct

[1] William Glasser, *Reality Therapy* (New York: Harper & Row, 1965), Chapter One.

when they are in pain is to have an adult take care of it for them. If the pain is a toothache, this expectation is a reasonable one—you take the kid to the dentist. But if the pain comes from depression, acting out, psychosomatic illness, or some other symptom that indicates a child has given up (renounced responsibility), then the last thing to do is try to remedy it yourself or to "call in someone to fix it."

We saw (in Chapter 3) that the mistake that Jack, the father of Billy, made was to imagine that an expert could inject responsibility into his son as if it were penicillin. Ultimately, Billy would have to begin to assume responsibility for his own actions. Obviously, in his case, this could not happen immediately. Nonetheless, the whole purpose of the previous chapter on love was to provide the parent with insights and advice about the first step toward building strength in a child. It is on the basis of this strength which is anchored in love that the child can and will learn to assume responsibility for himself. But he must be given the opportunity. In other words, no matter how tempted you may be to intervene in the child's problems and stress, avoid doing so. You can talk with him or her, offer counsel and advice, but *do not solve the problem for him*. If you do, he will learn that every time something goes wrong an older person will make the difficulty go away magically. This can only result in postponing the eventual reckoning with accountability and render the moment many times more trying.

With this in mind, let us move on to the more structured ways in which an adult can assist a young person to learn the slow lessons of responsibility (for no child can be expected to learn responsibility entirely on his own or simply because he is lucky enough to have loving parents). Before doing so, however, I would like to revert to a theme that was stressed earlier and will occur again: the importance of the example set by the parents. What it means here is that in considering how to teach your child responsibility, you would do well to consider just how responsibly you act, particularly in stressful situations.

For instance, how do you deal with the frustrations of driving a car? If someone cuts in front of you, do you fly off the handle, screaming and yelling and raising a fist at the offending vehicle? If you do, and your child catches you in the act, should you be surprised when he throws tantrums on the floor because something or someone provokes him? Similarly, if you blame circumstances and other people for your failures, can you expect your teen-age son or daughter, in spite of your sermons about "taking responsibility," not to do likewise?

This chapter is, in many ways, then, a primer on child-counseling for the parent.[2] The first stage of counseling, or responsibility training, is, as we saw in the last chapter, love. The crucial, initial advantage that a loving relationship with your child gives you, is access to him even when the going is rough. *Anytime a child sincerely believes an adult cares about him and is trying to help him, then the adult has access to the child.* This is not only true for the child/adult or child/parent relationship, by the way. It is the workable axiom in mental hospitals, schools, and correctional facilities— in all places where helping plays a central role.

Having access to a child will permit you to counsel him during those moments of difficulty when he has to face the truth, make decisions, confront complications and challenges, and deal with the consequences of his behavior. In fact, it is precisely at such moments when the lessons of responsibility are best taught and learned.

The second stage (after access) in counseling is to talk to the child who is encountering stress about *what he is doing here and now.* This is more difficult than it sounds. Children, like the rest of us, tend strongly to protect themselves, their egos, from the truth. There will be an almost irresistible inclination to get bogged down in a swamp of buck-passing, rationalizations, explanations, or discussions and squabbles about past behavior. The real key here is to cut away all ex-

[2] Based on William Glasser, *The Identity Society* (Rev. Ed.) (New York: Harper & Row, 1972, 1975).

cess verbiage with the scalpel of noncritical firmness: "Luke, I'm not concerned with why you did this; I'm not blaming you for it. I simply want you to tell me clearly: What are you doing?" I stress the noncritical attitude at this point because if you come on in an accusatory fashion, you'll frighten the child into hiding behind excuses, and you'll never get him to clear his brain of emotion and to observe lucidly.

Excuses are the enemy. Simply make it clear from the start that you neither ask for nor accept them. Try as much as possible to exclude excuses and their progeny (rationalizations, ex post factos, pleas, defenses, extenuations, and apologies) from the entire effort, so that the child won't even be tempted to have recourse to them. Not only are they antithetical to the whole process of teaching responsibility; they can do a great deal of harm in their own right. Excuses are costly in terms of time; they can destroy a relationship between child and adult (or husband and wife, therapist and client, for that matter) faster than almost anything else.

Now, by "excuses," I don't mean the small, unavoidable obstacles and impediments of daily life. If the young person is a few minutes late because he was delayed in traffic, and if tardiness is not a chronic problem with him, simply overlook it. But the big excuses offered when something important is not done usually start like: "Gee, Dad, let me explain why I didn't—." Exclude them right from the start. Excuses are the lepers of the modern world.

Unfortunately, however, excuses play a larger role in our society than lepers played in the ancient or medieval world. Indeed, excuses are a veritable pillar of the body politic. Look at the social upheaval of the mid- and late-sixties when it became clear that this country was suffering from inequities and prejudice. The government appointed all manner of "blue ribbon" panels to look into the causes and background of the situation, but then either the panel came up with no positive suggestions for change, or their advice, when offered, went unheeded by government. The entire effort, in other words, was a token, an excuse for inaction.

The same is true of a household and children. (What is government anyway but a reflection of the people for whom it stands?) When something goes wrong—when your child is arrested for trafficking in dope, for example—there is a lot of handwringing and ex post facto explanations which seem, intentionally or not, to replace hardheaded focusing on what to do now.

The child has four classic refuges as he retreats down the road (fighting a rearguard action every foot of the way) toward clearly observing and taking responsibility for his behavior. The first refuge is the Pit of Why, which is characterized by a very unprepossessing and beckoning entrance: "Will you just listen while I tell you why I couldn't study for the exam? See, this kid borrowed my book . . . etc." Before you know it, you're in the Pit. The only apparent way out—listening patiently to further discourses on why—is in reality the path to nowhere, to boredom and helplessness. Agreeing to discuss *why* only lends authenticity to, and consecrates with time and concern, the child's excuses. At this stage, *why* isn't important.

(Obviously there are many times and circumstances when an excuse is legitimate, but I'm not concerned with legitimacy here. The point now is this: dwelling on an excuse of *why,* even when it is fair and just, only makes it easier for the child to give up, absolve himself of responsibility, and find a way out. Any person who has accomplished a pioneering achievement in any field could give you ten thousand good reasons *why* such and such an idea wouldn't work. But they didn't think about them. They concentrated on finding a way that did work.)

Even if we were able to avoid or extricate ourselves from the Pit, we can't afford to overlook the next danger along the way: the Slough of the Past. In this vast nether region dwell all manner of ghosts and shadows, wishes and hurts, hopes and fears, excuses and explanations, facts and fancies that have very little, if any, *useful* bearing on the problem at hand. The Past is generally an event or a person to which the child (or adult) refers as a means of explaining away responsibility in the now, or of resisting pressures to change his behavior. "We moved to a new town when I was in the fourth grade and I was resentful of that move, and ever since then I've hated school and refused to work at it," is a typical example of a high schooler's invocation of the Past as self-exculpation.

The Past need not be uniformly excluded from counseling. For one thing, the Past certainly exerts a strong influence on the present and the future. For another, it can furnish the best examples of a person's behavior patterns, both positive and negative, and can enlighten him about his current actions and suggest ways to alter or modify them. What must be discouraged, however, is a child's taking refuge in the Past as a means of avoiding responsibility and discovery. It is a question of attitude and motivation. When the child seems genuinely willing to move ahead and understand what he is doing, that is the time to permit, even encourage, him to unburden himself of a memory (conscious or unconscious) that seems to be holding him down. Under these circumstances, however, the parent and counselor should urge the young person not to overvalue the memory he has uncovered, nor to allow it to weigh him down further. Let me reiterate, though, that in a society such as ours, merinated in cocktail-party Freudianism, there will be a strong tendency among pseudo-sophisticated teen-agers to ape their parents' readiness to explain away responsibility by reference to long-distant events. This should not be tolerated.

The Morass of Feelings, the third hazard on the path to responsibility, catches up counselors and parents in a lot of flypaper: "I didn't feel good in school, so I couldn't work." "Mr. Egret bores me, so I hate English." "I don't feel like practicing piano tonight." "I dunno, I just don't like getting up early. I'm no good in the morning." Etc. Feelings usually arise out of a child's behavior; they are the signals that tell him what response his actions or words are eliciting within him.

The prevalent feelings of boredom, sloth, passivity, the wish for immediate gratification, impatience, inadequacy, loneliness, and insecurity which pervade so many young people reflect their range of behavior: narrow. The way out from feelings of inadequacy and loneliness, for example, isn't to analyze those feelings to death, but to begin initiating behavior that will alter a person's life (which, in turn, will alter his feelings). The road away from boredom and passivity lies only in the direction of doing things, of activity. Granted, taking any one of these roads obviously risks antagonizing or exacerbating the feelings connected with the previous lifestyle. Because, in the beginning particularly, the young person will be a prisoner of his mind and hyperactive feelings, the counseling process must firmly bypass them and show them up for what they are: distracting obstacles.

(Again a disclaimer: I'm not saying feelings are unimportant or to be totally ignored. I'm saying, rather, that there is relatively little to be done about them, per se. Feelings are in the long run the by-products of behavior and behavior patterns, and the best way to deal with them, or change them, is not to discuss and analyze the feelings, but to alter or initiate behavior. This is easier said than done because feelings and emotions, more than anything else, distract the counselor and counselee. At their strongest, they are simply too potent to be ignored or skirted or even dealt with in any but a direct way. But always keep in mind the origins of these diverting clouds of smoke, and remember where the fire is.)

Frequently when the subtler variations and gambits of Why, Past and Feelings don't work, the child will brazenly take a final refuge in the Forest of Others. This Forest is a wondrous and wonderful place for the fleeing child because its thousands of trees can at any moment lift their boughs and open their branches to a sore-beset refugee. "All the teachers at this school are lousy." "But my mother wants me to be a cheerleader!" "Yeah, but all the other kids are smoking pot." "That coach doesn't like me, so he cut me from the team."

Do you see what I mean? The child's little tree becomes lost in the massed presence of so many other trees: parents, friends, teachers, coaches, and so on. The reason nothing ever gets done is always related to somebody else's problems, behavior, demands, expectations, hopes, and wishes. Youngsters of all ages make use of this refuge; indeed, they seem to have infallible compasses when it comes to finding the Forest of Others. The job of the parent-as-counselor is once again to be firm. He should reverse the old adage about not seeing the forest for the trees—saying to the child, in essence, you can't see *your* tree for the forest.

In one or all of the classic refuges, the parent must not get bogged down and thus distracted from the task at hand: getting the child to see what he is doing. The effect of these refuges is to toss the problem from the child's lap elsewhere—onto others, the past, emotions, etc. Eventually, though, if the adult permits these excuses and ploys to go unchecked and unchallenged, the real recipient of the passed buck will be the parent himself. This is bound to happen because the parent will become increasingly involved in trying to answer and solve the myriad objections, excuses, and explanations served up by the child. After a while, in a disconcerting way, the exasperated parent will find himself breathless and frustrated, the victim of reversed tables. The problem will now be *his*—how do I solve all my child's problems?—instead of the child's. Time and again I've seen parents and counselors have the tables reversed as a clever, sad, excuse-prone youngster spins his web of words and emotion around the sympathetic but naïve listener.

Thus, the parent-as-counselor can never forget this cardinal truth: *the problem is his, not mine.* Ultimately I can only *help him* to arrive at a solution. The burden—like the weakness, pain, and stress which created the burden—must be shouldered by the child. I can help him to do this, but I cannot carry it for him. Therefore, throughout this kind of therapeutic discussion, keep asking the question: What are *you* doing, my son (or daughter)? The parent may listen sympathetically, make sug-

gestions and offer advice occasionally as needed, even preach
a bit (though don't deceive yourself that it does much good);
but ultimately it all comes down to getting the child to take responsibility himself. And this can happen only if the child first
confronts the question of *what he is doing.* Sooner or later the
meaning and significance of that question will dawn on his
mind. Your job is to hang in there, resolute and single-
minded, until that happens.

In working with a young person there is a useful technique
that I know from firsthand experience for ensuring that he as-
sumes the full measure of responsibility for his actions. The
method is called the "I-statement," and it is simple, but highly
effective if used unrelentingly. Children, like the rest of us,
have a strong tendency to avoid the vertical pronoun (I) in
favor of "they," "he," "it," "one," or any other serviceable subject that will shift the initiator of action from the speaker to
some absent third party. It is a classic way of dodging one's
freedom: "Well, *we* were all out together and *we* got into a bit
of trouble," or *"Ya* know what it's like when *you've* been
drinking a bit too much," or *"One* simply doesn't know what
to do when *one* is in that sort of a situation," etc. As soon as
you hear the telltale sound of subject-shift, gently say to the
speaker: "I am not interested in what your friend, or brother,
or 'they' or 'one' are doing. They may have problems, but
they are not here; *you* are. I am only interested in what *you*
are doing." The trick here is to keep at the child, because very
quickly he will revert back to the shift, won't one?

Once you have got the child to look at what he is doing, it is
possible to move ahead to the next lesson of responsibility: *Is
what you are presently doing helping you?* If the child does
not first have a full, accurate picture of his behavior, then
broaching this question won't serve either of you very well. If,
on the other hand, he does have this picture, then he is in a position to make a judgment about that behavior. *Now, but not
before, a judgmental or critical attitude can come into play,
but it must be the child's, not the adult's.* His condemnation

(or celebration) of his own actions will mean a hell of a lot more to him than yours. In fact, it is at this moment of evaluation that internal strength begins to build.

A variation of the "Is it helping you?" question, which is particularly useful with hardheaded cases, is the reformulation: "What is the price you are paying for that behavior?" If asked with dispassionate curiosity so that the child detects no built-in prejudice in the questioner against his present behavior, he may be inclined to lay it all out at this point. As the steepness of the price gradually becomes clear to him, his willingness to go on paying it declines rapidly.

After all, what motivates people to change? The obvious answer is *pain*. The pain of "x" action becomes increasingly unbearable until it outweighs the superficial pleasure, so we finally renounce the behavior. But usually it's not so simple. Most of the time, the tie between a child's actions and the consequences (and pain) of those actions is not self-evident. Through careful questioning you will nudge the child into seeing the (often complicated) causal network between certain behavior patterns and the long-term consequences. *This* is the price he is paying, and it may well prove too high.

(Once in a while, the child will decide the price isn't too high after all. In that case, *he has accepted responsibility for his actions,* so, even if you disagree with his judgment, you have won the larger point. I have seen teen-agers decide to continue smoking pot or taking drugs, despite the fact that they know the risk they run with the law. In a couple of cases it took arrest and conviction of a felony before the price became too high. But that was *their* business and *their* choice. Mine was to get them to take responsibility, and they did.)

Let's take the case of Terry, fourteen years old. She's reached a point in life where new people, ideas, and alternatives are confronting her. She has always been a good student, a gifted equestrian, a popular leader. Now, as she enters high school, she is exposed to people who bad-mouth her traditional values, activities and friends, and substitute for them a whole range of new ones: smoking pot, popping pills, drinking, staying out late, cynicism, rebelliousness, sexual promiscuity.

Gradually, the consequences begin to make themselves felt in Terry's life. Her grades decline, her standing with her teachers and some of her former friends falls off, her attention to her previously much-loved horse becomes periodic. Terry herself is bewildered, surprised, angry, confused. Her new friends not only mean something to her, they provide ready-made excuses for why things are going badly in her life: "Your folks are riding your case." "Why do you have to please them by getting good grades?" "You're too old to be riding horses." "Your old friends are goody-goodies."

Terry, in her emotion-clouded state, is probably not able to easily see things the way they are in her life. She may be unaware that she is trying to live two different lifestyles and that the effort is breaking her. The job of a sincerely loving parent is not to march in with jackboots and outlaw all the new forms of behavior—that would only reinforce them in Terry's mind. Rather, the girl needs to see for herself the complex interrelationship among the sources of pleasure, pain, satisfaction, and frustration in her life. In other words, she has to see exactly how her actions are affecting her life. Until she does so, she is in no position to be able to evaluate the extent of her responsibility in these matters, the price she is paying for her behavior, and the decisions she must make to reduce the pain, confusion, and frustration.

If the parents cannot unemotionally and fairly lead Terry through step two, then they should call in a friend or therapist or teacher who can do so. Moreover, the parents *must* be prepared to live with the fact that *very likely* Terry's final observation of her complex life may lead her to different evaluations and choices from the ones her parents want for her. For example, she may decide that, after all, she really was grubbing for grades just to please external authorities; or that she no longer loves riding the way she did at age ten. She may also decide that some of the values she has encountered through her new friends—a critical outlook, a wider appreciation of lifestyles, an increased sense of freedom, etc.—are ones she wishes to keep.

The point is, whatever genuine strengths and values Terry had in her previous life are ones she will ultimately retain in her new life. Her parents can trust this fact. Their job is not to live Terry's life for her, but to get Terry to live her own life, taking responsibility for her choices, understanding where they lead, and making decisions for behavior that will reduce her present pain. If this process can be accomplished—i.e., if Terry learns the fine, hard art of self-observation and responsibility— then whatever life throws at her will ultimately redound to her benefit as a source of strength.

When it is clear that the child understands and accepts the fact that his current behavior in specific patterns and situations requires changing, he has arrived at the heart of the matter of responsibility; drawing up a detailed plan for meliorative, corrective action. A warning, however: plans may be made, but changes will happen only if the child himself truly wants to change and is not merely echoing his parents' wishes. At this point the plan need not contain all the seeds of a systematic transformation of a young person's life; rather, it need only be a feasible, practical design that will relate closely to the observed behavior of the child and will *begin* the process of changing it.

Now is when the experience and broader knowledge of the parent play a crucial, sometimes decisive role. Many parents don't know how to make plans. They either content themselves with procuring misty promises from a teary-eyed youngster, or they exact commitment to an entirely unworkable project. Valiant but vague vows like "I'm *never* going to fight with Mommy again" or "I'm going to get straight A's from now on" don't do any good for the child; in fact, they do harm because they are quickly broken and the child thereby begins to imagine that promises and plans *never* work.

So the first criterion of *a good plan is that it be workable within the strength of the child, that it be small enough so that the child can succeed.* His experience of succeeding will prove more important in the long run than whatever change the pain itself initially introduces into his life. For then the child will know that willed human effort toward a desired goal is possible and useful. He will have a feel for his own will, hence a sense of responsibility. Each success will reinforce his strength and self-confidence for the creation of larger, more important plans.

Thus, if the child's problem is that he is flunking math because he doesn't understand it and is doing no work, the plan should not be to work two or three hours a night toward making A's and B's on coming exams. My son Thomas, when he was nine, had trouble with arithmetic. At first I couldn't get him to accept a plan that involved homework at all. So we agreed to play Blackjack every night for fifteen minutes. The boy was delighted with the game, delighted to succeed at a plan of his own devising, and his facility with numbers improved. After a month or so, he was doing his arithmetic homework by himself, and his grades improved. (Note: this plan had the side effect of increasing the time we spent together in an enjoyable way.)

Second, *plans should be detailed and concrete, not indefinite or abstract.* The more you break something down into bite-size chunks, the better the chance that someone can assimilate it. A detailed plan gives a child many handles to get hold of; a vague one does not. Promising to be "nice" means nothing; it admits of too many excuses, interpretations, and empty gestures. This would be like telling a group of actors the general qualities and moods that a scene demands without giving them the dialogue. Thus, let me urge the parent not to be satisfied with "harder," "better," "nicer," and so on. See to it that the plan spells out the changes in behavior which such adjectives imply. For example, when homework is part of a plan, it must be decided *where* the child will do it, *with whom* he will do it, *when* he will do it, *how* he will do it, *what* he will do—all these details are critical to making a plan.

Third, *plans should be positive, not negative.* Negative fulfillment simply doesn't taste as sweet in the mouth as positive. More importantly, negative plans don't give much direction. If I said to you, "Reader, stop sitting down," would you know what to do? No, you'd only know what not to do. Okay, so that's a simplistic example. But what about the child who promises to stop being cranky? That's not a bad promise; it might even be do-able; but wouldn't it be better expressed and acted upon if you outlined four or five positive things the child could do that would obviate crankiness and replace it with something better?

Fourth, *plans should include the opportunity for repetitive behavior.* Ever since Freud, psychology has had a heyday showing the unfortunate consequences of repetitive behavior which reinforces negative compulsions. Well, why not turn the principle around and use it to our benefit? One rose does not a summer make, and neither does one successful action establish a good habit. The effect is cumulative; hence, the action must be repetitive.

Finally, plans should include the strong possibility of help and involvement of the parent; and in return for this, it should exact from the child a formal promise of willingness to work at the plan. Fulfilling a commitment to changed behavior will prove difficult for the child, and he will need the extra strength of having an adult around in those moments when he is working at the plan. If the plan involves renewed effort at difficult schoolwork, then perhaps the adult could be present in the room and willing to help while the young person plugs away at the algebra or grammar. If the plan focuses on altering the child's behavior toward teachers and classmates in situations where obviously the parent cannot be present, then the adult should see to it he is available for occasional or regular short evening discussions when the child can report on his day's success or failure at the plan. In sum, the child's desire to work at change is linked very tightly to nourishing, and potentially enjoyable, social contact with his parents. If the parents make a maximum effort to ground the plan with their presence and support, success will be all the more likely.

The young person's promise, though, is pivotal. Promises mean less today than they once did perhaps, but the fact remains that throughout three thousand years of Western history, vows and agreements have been symbols of a man's strength and honor and involvement with his fellow men. To a child, a promise may entail a purely symbolic gesture such as shaking hands, making a solemn oath or signing a written pledge (perhaps a copy of the plan itself). It may entail a more practical measure such as agreeing to call you, or speak to you, at certain stages in the plan's fulfillment. One youngster I was working with in private practice used to call me every evening to say that he had done his homework. This was an expression of his promise and it served an important function until the child's momentum was strong enough for him to suggest that the telephone calls cease.

So much, then, for the elements of a good plan. But what do you do if a stubborn child won't come up with a plan or won't take any of your suggestions for creating one? Children can be expert at showing you why nothing you offer is workable. In my experience the best thing to do at this point is to throw the whole burden back on their shoulders. "Okay, then, Nelson, I'm all out of ideas. I don't know what to do." The critical underlying message of this statement is this: *The problem, finally, my son, is yours, not mine.* One of the greatest errors of psychotherapists has been to assume the burden of the client's problem as if it were their own. The client is then free to sit back and watch while the therapist struggles through the contortions and pyrotechnics of some new formulation or suggestion or explanation. This is the reverse of what therapy should be. *Therapy should never for one moment allow the client to forget that the responsibility belongs to him.*

Getting back to the stubborn child who shoots down all your advice and plans, you need not fear that the candor of the statement "I don't know what to do" will destroy your contact with the young person. You don't lose people that easily, especially if you have proven to them your own sincerity, compassion, and presence. What you have shown dramatically with this statement is that the child, not you, is now suffering the consequences of his very stubbornness, that his behavior and words function like a reflexive verb in throwing the action and consequences back upon the subject.

If the child is equally sincere, and if you and he have really succeeded in getting him to take a hard look at his behavior, then the truthfulness of your confession should blast him out from behind this last defensive fortification he has erected. The ball is now in his court. Let *him* come up with some suggestions for a plan. The actions that ensue from his plan will very probably turn out to be the ones you had hoped for (and if they're different, but still wise and workable, good for him), but they'll have the added voltage of having come from the child.

In concluding this chapter, let me pass on to the reader one of the best techniques I've heard of for defusing a child's attempts to scrap a plan once it's been drawn up. The method is called "sabotage," and it has a wonderful way of plundering the treasure house of secret defenses and excuses before the guards know what's happened. In "sabotage" you ask the child to contemplate for a moment the full measure of this awesome plan he has devised. When he has done so and is wreathed in smiles, ask him the following question: "Now, then, what would be the very best, most effective ways you could imagine to make sure that this plan *does not get put into effect?*"

I have asked that question at least a hundred times, and each time it evokes an initial response of utter amazement and disbelief. You have to repeat it a few times before the child

catches on; you might even have to help him out a bit with
suggested answers. But very soon there follows a torrent of
words as the child informs you of the brilliant, cunning, and
efficacious means at his disposal for nullifying his own plan.
When he is finished, there may be another moment of shock
and silence (the guards have awoken to find the prize mare
has bolted), and then maybe a sheepish smile or two as the
child sees what he has done to himself. A loving hug might be
in order at this point.

CHAPTER 5

Discipline

In nature there are neither rewards nor punishments—there are consequences.

Robert Green Ingersoll

Punishment is one of the great traditional bulwarks of our society. It appears less in the home today than it did fifty years ago, but the concept of punishment still underlies our penal system (and for that matter, a good part of our military philosophy as well).

Socially, punishment is an anachronism. It was the hallmark of a society motivated by the need to survive and the wish for security. A world where survival and security are the principal goals is a world that can be controlled by fear, the fear of losing what is regarded as indispensable. Before unions were organized and powerful, and before the welfare state existed, a worker lived in desperate fear of the punishment of losing his job, because loss of his job could mean that he and his family might starve. Responsibility meant obedience to externally imposed rules. Punishment (though I strongly suspect it never worked as well as its exponents believed) probably proved a generally effective means of changing (or, rather, containing) undesirable behavior. It constituted such a direct threat to survival or security that its message could not be ignored.

That era is gone, even though many of its social/political/judicial/religious institutions still exist. Today the motivating drive for most Americans is no longer tied merely to the basics of food, clothes, shelter, and work. The postwar affluence of the United States has provided its citizenry with the luxury of new, more abstract goals: finding one's identity, expressing one's freedom, and, above all, *being happy*. This is part of the reason why the whole concept of responsibility has undergone a reformulation. It now revolves around the self—being responsible as a means of solidfying one's identity or achieving contentment or building satisfying relationships, all of which has to be learned.

The traditional rationale behind punishment is thus no longer valid. In a culture not oppressed by fear, punishment loses what little bite it had. No longer do people conform or change merely because of rules, deterences, threats; instead, internal motivation has become equally, if not more, important. When rehabilitation, personal happiness, social justice, and internal responsibility figure among the key goals or myths of a society, then punishment becomes dysfunctional in achieving them, whatever effectiveness it may have had when the goals and myths revolved around survival and security.

In any case, most of the people upon whose heads real punishment is visited these days are the weak—poor people, racial minorities, people without confidence, without love, without worth or hope. When they break the rules of the strong—which is to say, the rules of society which the strong have created—they are punished on the assumption that punishment will induce them to change. But the assumption is false. Where punishing the strong *might* induce change, or at least deterence (though it is by no means the best way of doing so), punishing the weak only increases their weakness because it doesn't show them *what to do*. It doesn't teach them how to acquire those qualities of personal responsibility—coping strength, confidence, and worth—that society requires. It merely increases their pain and their anxiety to be rid of pain—anxiety which only leads them to strike back at society. The

violence of the weak, indeed, is now so pervasive and horrify-
ing that you would think we'd develop some better means than
punishment for coming to grips with it.

On the individual level, punishment means harming a person physically or verbally. With children, it means that when
your child sasses you back at the dinner table you slap him in
the face; when he says something foolish you mock or humili-
ate him. That's punishment. So are paddling children, depriv-
ing them of food, suspension, detention, deprivation of choice
and human love, and so on. The armory of traditional punishment is well stocked. But such reactions, as I have said, do not
teach responsibility or promote the acquisition of coping
strength in a child.

A modern counterpart of the evil of punishment is *protectiveness*. Protectiveness is possible only in a society of
affluence, indulgence, momism, and permissiveness. Applied
to young people, it is essentially the wish to insulate them from
all painful contact with reality, even when it means protecting
them from the unhappy consequences of their own actions. As
such, it obviously runs directly counter to the requirements of
teaching responsibility.

My personal *bête noire* is the protective mother who rushes
to school whenever her child receives a low grade to blame the
teacher for upsetting Johnny. Each time this happens, her
son's sense of autonomy is diminished and his vision of reality
is distorted by the amniotic fluid of his mother's actions. (Amniotic fluid is what surrounds the child in the womb and in-
sulates it from the jolts and bumps of the outside world.)

You can multiply this example by hundreds. I remember a
good-looking eighteen-year-old named Jeff, who was sent to
my office by his father because the boy was on drugs, had been
in trouble with the law, and was generally an undependable,
selfish, moody young man. To this day, I recall the smug, callous smile on Jeff's face as he talked about how he had
"dodged the pen" through his father's expensive lawyer and his

contacts in the upper echelons of local government. The boy drove a late-model sports car, held no job, drew an outsized allowance, and lived in his parents' home, where he had a three-room suite all to himself.

As we sat and talked, Jeff suddenly propositioned me: how would I like to give him five dollars for gas for his car in return for his coming to see me three more sessions? In many years of teaching and practice, I thought I had plumbed the depths of teen-age cynicism, but Jeff's "offer," as he called it, disgusted me. I replied that I had no objection to his getting a job to earn gas money, at which point the boy got up and walked out of my office. I immediately called his father, the president of a large corporation in our area, and asked him to come in for a talk.

The following day the father arrived looking rather tired. He later admitted he had been "up half the night" driving sixty miles to pick up Jeff, who had run out of gas. I explained to the man that I could do nothing for Jeff; so far there was no reason for the boy to want to change, protected as he was by his father's money and connections. How could you teach responsibility to someone who had so little apparent need for it? But I did warn the man that eventually his best efforts to insulate his son would not suffice to prevent Jeff's harsh confrontation with reality. It was merely a question of when.

The parents' role is to prepare their children for life, not insulate them from it. Why send your son to a Reality Therapist if your own actions permit him to live in an illusion? Just as punishment was the perverted expression of the survival society, so protectiveness is a reflection of our affluent society's wish to give strength to our children without their having to work for it.

We who have made such astonishing progress in harnessing nature and eradicating disease, mistakenly assume we can employ our pain-saving devices in the far more inaccessible realm of personality. What we must realize is that our material affluence and technical control have merely freed society from one type of conflict in order to face other, less tangible challenges where the same methods, concepts and wealth are of no help, but indeed a hindrance.

So what is the best route between the Charybdis of punishment and the Scylla of protectiveness? As far as I can see, the best path lies in the direction of discipline. And by discipline I mean *allowing the child to accept responsibility for what he does and experience the natural or social consequences of his actions.* Put another way, it is teaching children to obey the "rules." Where punishment creates unnatural and cruel consequences for the child's actions, protectiveness robs him of both responsibility and consequences. Discipline permits direct contact with stressful reality, which can only increase the child's strength for coping and opportunity for growth.

Discipline, in the way we are using the term in this chapter, *only* applies when the child has violated the rights of others or the rules of family, society, or nature. I stress the word only, because parents and teachers may be quick to discipline young people in areas where it doesn't apply. For example, if a child isn't doing his homework, or if he reneges on a plan to which he's committed himself, this isn't *prima facie* evidence to discipline him. What is required is to continue to apply the steps outlined in Chapters 3 and 4 and allow him to live with the consequences of his negligence or laziness. The child is only harming himself, which is punishment enough. The parent needn't add his bushel.

If the child is preventing others from doing their homework, however, or if his actions violate the rules of the home in which he lives, then discipline (i.e., experiencing the foreordained, accepted consequences of his action) is in order. Speaking of rules, the fewer the better. Rules should also be reasonable, equitable (applying equally to everybody), and, most important, flexible. Rules are not graven on stone tablets; they can change, and the child should know that he has some voice in changing them. This is not to say a child should make

the law, or even that his input should equal that of his parents
—only that he has the right to discuss rules as they apply to
himself.

I recall once that my daughter Mary Ellen, then age fifteen,
was going out for the evening. The standing rule of our house
was that she must be home by eleven o'clock. She told me that
the party in question was an important one to her, and asked if
I would leave it to her discretion to remain there an extra hour
if she so chose. I answered yes, only requesting that she call
me and tell me when and how she would be getting home.

Assuming that discipline is in order, what specifically do
you do? Well, the first thing is to take a hard look at what you,
the parent, are doing and feeling. Are you raising your voice?
Do you pick on your child? Have you been spending enough
time with him lately? Are you tempted to be punitive? Might
there be some legitimate extenuating circumstances in this instance? In other words, if you're going to start disciplining the
child, you've first got to put your own house in order and
make sure you are calm and have done everything you're responsible for doing.

By the way, while you're quickly scanning your own behavior and running down the list of "do's" and "don'ts," try to
remember that after-the-fact criticism is not very useful and is
always painful for the child. If you have to criticize, do it in
ways and in situations where he can do something about it.
Otherwise, the effect of the criticism will only further reduce
the child's ability to do the right thing. Any good coach knows
enough not to dwell on past errors, but to look toward the future. "Okay, let's try it again in a better way" is the best
attitude.

Ideally, the next step is to talk to your child, although this
may not be possible if both of you are standing knee-deep in a
flood of emotion. *Never* try to talk to a child when you or he
are under the rancorous dominion of feelings. Mind, intelligence, wisdom have no voice that can be heard over the shouts

of anger, hurt, pain. The best thing to do under the circumstances is *calmly, nonpunitively to tell him to go to his room until he is ready to talk reasonably.* With a very young child, you may have to firmly but gently take him to his room.

What you have done is preserve the young person's *capacity for choice* as well as reduce the perimeter of his social contact to a dimension he can safely handle. The natural consequence of his disruptive, rule-breaking behavior has been that he must be separated from the rest of the family, but you are leaving with him the decision to return when he feels ready. In other words, you have allowed the choice without which there could be no responsibility on his part.

If you send him to his room for a specified amount of time, which you, not he, determines, this action may appear to be quite similar to what I am advocating, but in fact the distinction is crucial: you will be leaving out the element of choice. For whatever period the child must stay in his room, he is without choice, hence (to some extent at least) without a feeling of personal responsibility. Moreover, you have no way of knowing whether the amount of time you specify is adequate. It may be too short, in which case the kid will return to the family too soon and probably blow up at the next stressful confrontation. Or, if the quarantine is too long, the child will sulk and see the action as punitive (i.e., you will be sequestering him from those he loves when he feels ready to be reconciled to them).

Sometimes with certain children, the scenario won't happen as swimmingly as I have indicated. A child might be acting disruptively, you send him to his room, and he doesn't come out. The disciplinary action doesn't mean anything, because the child may not see any value in coming out of his room. Life for him, inside or outside his room, is a painful or apathetic experience. In this case, restriction can be psychologically harmful. If your child is deeply withdrawn, you may have to help him "come out of his room." You will have to teach him involvement with you and with life in general. He needs to be shown that it's worthwhile to come out of his room, that there can be content in his life which he can value greatly.

In other words, and this is a *key* point, without the basis of a loving relationship, discipline does not work. Discipline is a means of teaching responsibility, but if a child doesn't have enough significant involvement with others to care about life, then the first thing to do is work on creating that involvement. *Nothing* else will work until it is there. This is a special case, however, though unfortunately an increasingly common one, and most of the time children do have enough involvement with life and people so that discipline will affect them.

Returning, then, to the previous discussion, let me reiterate that *choice always implies responsibility, and this is the key to discipline.* Control is something to be shared. The parent determines (with input from the child) the rules and the consequences of behavior. The child, however, controls his behavior and thereby the duration of the isolation or the types of restrictions his behavior may visit upon him. Parents who attempt to control and dominate too much of the child's life don't prepare him for the real world.

In the normal course of things, parents (especially fathers) spend very little time with their children; and the young people's choices of behavior when the parents are not around depend largely on how the children were trained. In the parent's absence, the child must know how to make decisions, assume responsibility, cope with stress. Thus, parents cannot afford the luxury of not preparing the child for the demands of the outside world. In all their dealings with their sons and daughters, including discipline, they dare not forget the crucial lessons of responsibility and choice.

Sometimes, too, parents can learn a lesson or two *from* their children. I remember a humorous occasion at dinner with my family that illustrates what I have been talking about in this section. My wife, Hester, and I were dining with our two youngest children, Thomas, age eleven, and Luke, age eight.

Halfway through the meal, my fourteen-year-old son Joseph came to the table. I yelled at him for being late, and Hester (who makes sure I practice what I preach) yelled at me for yelling at him. Whereupon Thomas looked up from his plate and said to his parents, "Go to your room and make a plan. Come back when you have it."

Sometimes the natural consequences of a child's misbehavior will include the withdrawal of privileges. If he is negligent or sloppy in his performance of the tasks and chores given to him around the home, then other people are obliged to take over his work and he is, in effect, violating their rights and freedoms.

Withdrawing privileges in the home is a reflection of what happens in society. If a sixteen-year-old abuses the privilege of driving by going too fast, the privilege will be taken away from him by the courts. If a child continually abuses the privilege of education, through disruptive actions, he will ultimately be required to withdraw from the school. If he traffics in dope, he risks losing a good deal more than a few privileges. The point is that the lesson of abuse and withdrawal should be learned early in the home, so that when the child is operating alone in the world, he will do so responsibly.

Sometimes, however, withdrawing privileges isn't always necessary in order to teach discipline. I have a good friend, Bob, who maintains very close relationships with his children. His fifteen-year-old son Tim has reached the age of motorcycle mania. He is a delightful lad—kind, thoughtful, responsible—but a while back his enthusiasm for the "bike" led him to drive the thing on a country highway, which is against the law until next year, when he is old enough to get a license. (The motorcycle is intended for desert and dirt riding only.) A policeman saw Tim on the road and turned on his flasher, but the boy became suddenly frightened and tried to flee. He only got about a hundred yards before he and the motorcycle careened into a clump of bushes. Tim wasn't hurt, but he got a good scare from the scolding the police officer gave him. Resisting arrest is a felony, and the officer advised Tim he was risking serious trouble with the law. He then brought the boy home and had a separate conversation with Tim's father.

Now, Bob is a good parent who believes unswervingly in the value of "natural consequences." With no rationalizations, after hearing the story, he said to the officer point-blank: "The boy clearly did it. Do you intend to book him?" The policeman said no. This was the boy's first offense. Tim was very polite (and looked very scared); there was no need to come down hard on him.

When the policeman left, Bob did not attempt to lecture his son. It was clear from Tim's subdued behavior and wet eyes that he was undergoing his own self-interrogation and was too emotion-filled to talk to his father. The next day, Bob went to his son and quietly asked him, "Do you know what a felony is and what it could do to your life to have one on your record?" The boy had an idea, but the father spelled it out for him a bit more. Then he asked Tim, "What do you plan to do?" Tim answered, "I plan to stick to the trails and never to try to outrun a cop again." That was the end of the affair. Bob did nothing more.

The point is, the father did not try to talk down or through the policeman, nor in any way interfere with the policeman's decision; nor on the other hand, did he threaten and hector his son or make arbitrary decisions about taking the motorcycle away from him. He didn't even tell the boy to go to his room. He simply trusted the boy's internal process. He suspected that Tim knew what he had done, understood the consequences of his actions and took responsibility for them. In other words, he knew that the lessons which discipline should teach were already being learned, and he didn't interfere with the situation by overlaying it with a useless coating of emotion, punishment, and lectures.

Discipline, thus, is not what you *do to* a kid; it's getting him to learn responsibility. If this larger goal is attained, there is no need for anything further. Had Tim continued to abuse the privilege of riding the cycle, it would then be clear he hadn't learned the lesson of responsibility after all, and it would have been necessary to take away the bike for a time. Fortunately, Bob had built a loving relationship with his son over the years, which allowed him to have confidence in his son's process.

Tim and Bob are admittedly ideal examples, but what if it doesn't go so well? What if the parent and child don't have a strong base of love, trust, and communication? What if sending a child to his room or taking away privileges are not effective? Well, it depends; there are no easy answers. If you can still talk to your child—that is, if there are still some shreds of a loving relationship—I would urge you to sit him down and say point-blank: "Look, Son, I really don't know what to do any more, it's beyond me. This is your life. You aren't hurting me nearly as much as you are hurting yourself." Sometimes this is effective, especially if the child is laboring under the illusion that he is blackmailing you with his self-destructive behavior. It might help, in other words, if he knows that you're not going to drown when he sinks his ship. Lastly, you might offer to call in a professional counselor or therapist—though only if the young person is willing to see him and work with him.

But if your involvement with the child is slight or nonexistent, and if the child steadfastly refuses your help and that of a professional, then you just have to rely upon the fact that when people (adults or children) persist in leading the wrong kinds of lives, reality will eventually bring them to their senses. I was seeing a fifteen-year-old boy for a number of weeks, but his behavior at home grew consistently worse. He drank heavily, stayed out late, was abusive to his stepmother, and made life intolerable for his stepsister. He also refused to participate in his sessions with me.

Finally I called in the father and told him I thought he was wasting his money by sending his son to me. The kid seem-

ingly had no intention of changing his behavior. I added that
in my experience either the father would *have* to spend more
time with the boy and try hard to develop a relationship with
him or his son would end up at the Ohio Youth Commission.
The father explained in great detail why he didn't have time.
Three months later the boy was picked up in a stolen car.

In other words, the answer lies in a process that begins long
before such a crisis reaches a head. As I have discussed in the
preceding chapters, when the child is very young is the time to
lay the foundations of love, worth, and responsibility. There is
no alternative to this, no gimmick or technique of punishment, protectiveness, or discipline that will get around it.
When the kid is already an alcoholic, an addict, a car thief, or
a self-centered, apathetic, callous boor, it's too late. If you ask
me then, "What do we do?" I have no immediate answer except to tell you to try hard to do those things you didn't do
before.

In conclusion, I guess I should hold out a bit of hope in the
form of a suggestion by my friend Alex Bassin: *Never Give
Up.* Only you the parent or teacher or counselor or friend can
decide when "never" is. For some people it's longer than for
others. Quite often when you are dealing with even the most
incorrigible of youngsters and are literally at your wits' end,
you'll find they get the message. (Sometimes they'll have got-
ten it long before this, but you won't know until later.) The
point is, by hanging on to your responsibility for your child
well past the point of reasonable human endurance, you'll be
setting an example of value to your child and to yourself.

CHAPTER 6

Work

There are, of course, the happy few who find a savor in their daily job: the Indiana stonemason, who looks upon his work and sees that it is good; the Chicago piano tuner, who seeks and finds the sound that delights; the bookbinder, who saves a piece of history; the Brooklyn fireman, who saves a piece of life. . . . But don't these satisfactions, like Jude's hunger for knowledge, tell us more about the person than about his task? Perhaps. Nonetheless, there is a common attribute here: a meaning to their work well over and beyond the reward of the paycheck.

Studs Terkel, *Working*

Sigmund Freud in an insightful moment (of which he had many) wrote that the two interwoven strands of a satisfying life are *love* and *work*. It was his dialectical understanding that we cannot really have one without the other. Yet in a society which traditionally escapes the drudgery and exploitation of work by fleeing to the arms of spouse, lover, girl- (or boy-) friend, or prostitute—or with children and friends; or in sports and leisure—the ideal interrelationship of love and work becomes the reality of antagonism, or at best, rivalry. We Americans today (and probably Russians and Icelanders as well) work because we have to; we love because we want to. The two activities go together about as comfortably as faith and doubt.

Yet I persist in believing Freud was right. To surrender the possibility of finding lasting, profound satisfaction in work (defined more broadly than simply the job) is to renounce half of what the human adventure is all about. Likewise, it's unfair to construe love as a refuge from work, instead of as a collaborator in the creation of a fulfilled life. By asking love alone to soothe our aches and fill our emptinesses, we are loading it with a burden it cannot carry. In doing so, we run the risk of seriously misconceiving the nature, purpose, and interrelationship of love and work.

One of the basic tenets of this book (and of Reality Therapy) is that the cornerstones of strength-building, whether in children or adults, are the feelings of love and worth. The absence of the former creates loneliness; of the latter, inadequacy. I have written about this in the preceding chapters; but what I have not made clear until now is the exact source of worth, or the way in which love and worth are inextricably bound. Very simply, *worth comes from work,* not work defined as merely the nine-to-five job you do (though this can be an important element of it), but *work in the larger sense of creative intellectual, artistic, and manual self-expression.* Work is the active intervention of human beings—through their minds, imaginations, hands—in nature and society. It is one of the key means by which we impose our will, our identity, our talent upon the world and people, whether it be planting a garden, reading to a blind person, fashioning a cabinet, training a horse, writing a book, producing a chemical reaction, or inventing an ambulatory module for scooping up dirt on Mars.

I realize that socially organized labor takes on assembly-line dreariness more frequently than it permits or elicits creative self-expression; and clearly much of the work-time of the average man, woman, and child is devoted to the urgent, oftentimes compulsive, pursuit of security, wealth, success, prestige, or any number of other goals, some of them noble, some ignoble. But this does not mean we should indiscriminately accept the shabby, distorted values, definitions, and idols of the marketplace and proclaim them to our children as the *only* truths, losing touch with what life could be, or losing faith in our children's ability to achieve a better life.

We all have daily jobs we *have* to do, and many of them aren't very romantic or high-falutin'. But nobody says you cannot find worth in the humblest of pursuits; indeed, the challenge of doing so might be one of the greatest challenges of our era. The larger point is this: whether it comes from your daily job, or from a hobby, or a pastime, we all need the feeling of worth that comes only from work in the fullest sense of the word.

If we don't have this feeling, it doesn't matter how much security we have or how much money we make. Neither one will make up for the emptiness deep down inside. It may be unrealistic, you'll say, to talk about work and worth in such glorious tones when the reality is so dismal. But isn't it *more* unrealistic to imagine you can get through life in a satisfying way without experiencing the worth that comes from work?

In any event, I think we would agree that children ought to know what work and worth *can* be, if only so that they can articulate to themselves the nature and meaning of some of their most profound inner strivings. To this end, we have to understand first that work means something different to young people today than it meant to the generation of parents who grew up in the thirties and forties. Whereas work for us was intimately interwoven with material security (and for some Depression-hit people, survival), it has different, more complex, less straightforward connotations for our children. They have been raised in a society of relative affluence, and we are irritated and offended by their insouciance toward money. But isn't it largely our fault (if "fault" is the word) for creating a world of such impregnable material safety? (Well, not quite impregnable, as we saw in the recession and stagflation of 1973–75.) As struggling parents, our main concern was to make sure our children wouldn't have to worry about where their next dollar was coming from. And now we fret and gnash our teeth because they don't know the value of a buck. Unwittingly we insulated them from the strain and struggle of the marketplace, and thus prepared them poorly for coping with stress of any sort.

Insulation from security fears is one side of the coin—and it describes well the contempt for materialism among the flower children and hippies of the mid- and late-sixties. But the other side of the coin is the success-obsessed offspring we have turned out (more numerous than the rebels), who march in serried ranks to college, then to joblessness and overqualification in a society which cannot accommodate their numbers or their expectations. These children and their frustrated hopes of "making it" are further from experiencing the worth that flows from authentic, creative work (and probably are potentially more socially explosive) than their hippie and dropout brothers and sisters, who at least may have opted out of a hopeless, unfulfilling rat race.

In any event, the point is this: the obsession that leads a child to devote his youth to work in order to win the external trappings of prestige and wealth is a caricature of work and worth; while opting out altogether and sinking into pot smoking, indolence or material indulgence (the spoiled kids who live only for their stereos, motorbikes, skis, and cars) are hardly better. I use the word "caricature" in its literal sense: each of these paths has taken one or two elements of work and blown it into the whole enchilada. The grinds have sunk their teeth into discipline and effort, while the opt-outs have basked in the pleasure element of work and reveled in personal choice. Each has a part of the truth about work; each probably experiences a distorted glimmer of worth. But each has something more to learn.

Let's see if we can dissect work, as we did love, in order to lay out its parts and see more clearly where worth that creates strength comes from. The categories I shall use will be the same as those for love: *effort, value, pleasure,* and *self-discipline.*

Effort is the most obvious ingredient in work, the sweat part —or, as one of my children put it, "Effort is the work part of work." Kids know what effort means—there's nothing subtle about it. Some youngsters put out, others don't. Effort is usually so clearly related to payoff or remuneration that the child can pretty easily gauge what is necessary. If he wants to play the piano well, or make enough money to buy a stereo, or get high grades in school, or make the tennis team, he has an idea of the kind of effort that will be required of him.

The job of the parent, besides setting an example by a consistent outlay of effort, is to support and encourage the child to exert effort. Effort brings stress, and the effort of work may figure among the first difficult stresses a child has to confront. When the child is young, the parent should be there not only to provide him with an opportunity for effortful work, but also to help him through the difficult initial experiences.

Effort will be the child's first glimpse of what is required to keep a family, a household, and a society functioning. It will also be his first glimpse of his own role in these processes. Thus I strongly urge parents to integrate a youngster from the time he enters kindergarten into the work-life of the family. I know some parents who, when the child is one or two years old, regularly ask him to "help Mommy pick up your toys." As the youngster gets older, he should be given certain minimum tasks around the house which are simply, naturally, completely his. Children should be expected as a matter of course to keep their rooms clean and their possessions (cars, bikes, motorcycles, stereos, clothes, or whatever) orderly and functional.

Looking back with the frustrating wisdom of hindsight, I wish I had given all my children further tasks in the household so that they would know from daily experience what it means to keep a family going. To the three boys still living at home I now assign various small tasks on a rotating basis—helping their mother in the kitchen, sweeping out the garage, taking out the trash, setting the table, etc.

This brings me to another point: the so-called appropriateness of having male children wash dishes and help with the cooking, or of asking young girls to help fix the car or clean the garage. The reader will make his own decision about these matters of course, but I think it is essential to remember that the world our children are living and growing up in is a world of radical redefinition (and not a moment too soon, in my opinion) of traditional gender roles.

Just on a simple, practical level, boys and men are increasingly expected to cook for themselves, watch the children, and wash the dishes, while girls and women had damn well better know about buying and fixing cars, getting jobs, and physically protecting themselves from assault. I, for one, advocate marrying this particular spirit of the times as early and joyfully as possible (though I recognize that some marriages are purely for convenience).

This discussion of expending effort in work would be incomplete without some mention of the ancient question of allowance. Wages, alms, bread, cabbage, handout, dough, call it what you will: it's *money*. Children and money: they go together like age and sex. The more you get of one, the less you have of the other. Like anybody else, children will invariably want money, and the parent should, insofar as he can, provide them with the chance to earn it around the house. It is obviously very much in the spirit of this book to state that a child's growth in responsibility and autonomy will be enhanced if he has a certain degree of financial independence.

The larger point here, however, is *not* that the child should become a successful capitalist before he is ten. On the contrary, I try hard to discourage my children from being obsessed with money. Fair remuneration for effort, though, can teach a child something (though not everything, by any means) about the worth that comes from work. The point is, there is a great deal of satisfaction and incentive in being financially rewarded for work done to the best of one's ability. The reward is an important (if by no means the only) element of worth. Moreover, having his own money will permit your child a degree of financial independence which, in turn, will teach him lessons he should know about the marketplace, particularly that mighty maxim of economic philosophy, capitalist or socialist: "There's no such thing as a free lunch." Simply giving a child money will teach him nothing except that he can get things for nothing and that people will always be doing things for him with no expectation of return—two unrealistic assumptions, to say the least.

Finally, there's one more reason why a child should have to earn his money. If you simply give it to him, a child may come to confuse receiving money with receiving love. But, in fact, the two things are totally different interactions. Showing love, by its very nature, refutes the payoff-reward schema; love is automatic and constant, the basis of your and your child's whole relationship. Money paid for work, however, is a specific interaction intended to teach a young person about responsibility and work and thereby instill in him elements of self-worth.

All these reasons are good ones for setting up some kind of work/pay system for your child from his earliest years—but the important reasons revolve around teaching responsibility and worth. Try to make certain that these concepts are not lost sight of in the headlong rush to accumulate dollars, for they, not the money, are the valuable goals.

I strongly believe that the virtues of work/pay must be heavily balanced by an awareness that money isn't everything. I disagree, for example, with the philosophy that a child must be taught to pay for *everything* he needs, including clothes and food (unless the family's financial circumstances require the child's assistance—which is a different matter). That kind of approach is the surest way to see to it that the child never goes beyond effort in learning about the elements of work, nor beyond financial reward in his feelings of worth. Thus, I have always made it a habit not to make a big deal over money and expenses. If a child is learning the true value of effort and reward, there's no need for you to feel qualms about occasionally helping him to meet various expenses, or about giving him presents from time to time.

As your child grows older, the possibility of taking a part-time job may arise. There is nothing wrong with holding a part-time job; indeed, much benefit can be derived from it. However, I urge the parent and the child to keep the broader goal and the nature of work in mind and not surrender them wholesale to the money-making mania. An outside job, in addition to earning dollars, can also teach the child something more about work and worth.

Several children I know didn't just circulate among the local merchants and retailers asking for clerk or sales positions; they created their own business on the basis of some skill or service they could provide (e.g., yard work and gardening, carwashing, housepainting, repair work, tutoring, etc.). The satisfaction and skill these children learned will not only increase their sense of responsibility, independence, and worth, but it will also one day make them much less dependent upon the employment office or upon welfare benefits than people whose only recourse is to apply for an existing job.

In conclusion, I would like to make one final point. Let the young person spend his money—whether earned directly or received as an allowance or as a gift—as he sees fit. If you disapprove, then bite your tongue or sit on your hands. Maybe buying a new stereo isn't as good a way to spend the money as saving it for college or a rainy day—but that's the child's business. He'll learn about priorities and about what's foolish and wise by making his own decisions. Remember, the basis of responsibility is the capacity to make choices—hence the need for freedom. Ensuring his freedom is far more important than intervening to "save" him from a stupid purchase.

The first dimension of work a child encounters while growing up is most often *effort*—because it's the most obvious. But shortly thereafter, while the child is still quite young, it is essential that he discover the most significant element of work: *value. Value can be defined as the meaning your work has, in your own eyes and in terms of its benefit to your fellow men.* In other words, it is at once the most personal and the most social aspect of human labor.

The *personal value* of your work is the degree to which it best utilizes your intelligence, creativity, imagination, talent, and/or manual dexterity, as well as your moral principles and your faith. In other words, how well does your work express accurately, satisfyingly, completely, the unique concatenation of talents, mind, principles, body, spirit, and skills that are you?

The alienated corporate executive, for example, is a stereotype of our time: the faceless man in the gray flannel three-piecer who feels locked into a job that provides little challenge or satisfaction, but who—whether from inertia, duty, or fear—sticks to his last. Some kinds of work seem inherently more attractive in terms of interest, personal meaning, and recognition, than others. Nursing, teaching, art, medicine, and architecture, for example, would probably seem preferable in terms of personal fulfillment than assembly-line toil or menial labor. Yet I have known many alienated and bored schoolteachers and social workers; and at a large midwestern steel mill, where I worked for a few years I met some industrial workers who derived considerable satisfaction from their labor. Personal value is obviously a personal question. But it is also an irreducible requirement for a satisfying work experience.

Much of the psychological alienation of our times stems from the fact that the work that many men and women do does not express even a small part of the workers' selves. On one level this is the responsibility of society and government, but on another level it is the responsibility of generations of men and women who grew up without learning the value of self-expression in work, or whose fears about security sapped their courage to the point where they traded their feelings of worth for material security.

If it were possible to live with this trade-off, it might be defensible on practical grounds, but in the long run it is unrealistic because the need for self-expression in work cannot be ignored forever. *The personal value of work, in other words, is not a luxury,* contrary to what is generally thought. If your daily work has little personal value, if it is abhorrent, boring, or unchallenging, no amount of success will stifle your need for worth forever. Eventually in your heart, in your happiness, in your self-image, and very likely in your relationships with people, this void, this unfulfillment, will make itself felt.

As indicated earlier, self-expression is only one half of work value—the personal half. *The other part is the benefit your labor has for your fellow men.* If human beings lived alone like so many islands in a dark sea, if they were psychologically, socially, and economically self-sufficient, and if men worked purely for their own satisfaction, expression, and survival, there would be no need for a wider definition of value beyond the personal dimension we have discussed. Such is most assuredly not the case. Since Aristotle, philosophers and writers of every school and opinion have described man's social nature and spoken of his interdependence. Psychologically, man's two greatest needs, love and worth, and the two activities to which they correspond, loving and working, presuppose *the presence of a community of fellow men.*

Thus, whether we like it or not, whether we admit it or not, we need our fellow men. We can have no love and no worth outside of the community. The great Dutch painter Vincent Van Gogh never sold a painting while he lived—and the stress of constantly confronting his fellow men's lack of interest in his work eventually drove him mad. He was a weak man, you'll say, and should have had greater confidence in himself. Heaven knows there were a few great artists, especially composers, who were unsuccessful in their lifetimes, yet didn't go mad. Just so. But if their courage and their confidence held, it was precisely because they believed that one day the world *would* recognize the *value* of their contributions to art and to their fellow men. Thus my point stands: the worth we derive from work is twofold, just as the value of work is twofold. On the one hand, our self-expression and satisfaction; on the other, the pleasure, the betterment, and the recognition of our fellows.

I stress this concept of *value*, both personal and social, in work, because we seem to have forgotten it in our workaday lives; hence, we do not teach our children, by example and word, the whole meaning of the work experience in life. Much of what men do neither satisfies them as individuals nor improves the welfare of the species. This is so often the case that I fear the simple, obvious points I am making may sound crazily utopian. Yet they are only the basic truths which are found in the philosophies, religions, and political treatises we profess to venerate.

What meaning do all these words about personal and social value have, on a practical level, with respect to raising kids? First of all, it means that *we can't afford to go on pretending to our children that the only, or even the main, function of work is to make money or be "successful."* If we do, we'll continue to turn out more alienated people who will sooner or later have to confront the results of their blindness to work value (both personal and social) in the form of unhappiness, psychological insecurity, urban blight, overproduction of useless commodities, etc.

Second, it means that *we should teach our children, from their earliest years, that work isn't only what you do at the office or at the plant.* Work in this larger sense plays a key role in maintaining the satisfaction and welfare of the family of which the child is a member. It has to do with the child's learning experience in school as well. In fact, after love, work is probably our most personal way of expressing ourselves. If the child knows that washing the dishes, cleaning out the garage, learning French, tutoring the neighbor's daughter in algebra, campaigning for a public official, and volunteering to read to a blind person, are *all* aspects of the human activity we call work, he will realize that payment in the form of money is only one reward and that work provides other, more important functions, goals, and rewards.

Third, to further expose the child to the breadth of work, I favor *involving him from a young age in the running of the family and in the work experiences of the parents.* It is not difficult to give him some role in the decision-making process of the family. He can learn how food is selected and purchased by occasionally accompanying his parents to the store. He can begin to understand the need for balancing the family budget by watching his father do it. He can participate in decisions about remodeling, decorating, or rearranging the furniture. All it requires of the parent is a little extra effort and patience to explain what they take for granted, to answer questions . . .

On another level, the child should know what kind of work his parents do, not simply that they are nurses, lawyers, or shop superintendents, but actually what they do and what impact their work has on society. My father often took me with him when he went to court (he was a county judge). I also accompanied him on political campaigns, and many Sundays I helped him count up the collection in our local parish church. In my practice now as a counselor, I strongly urge parents to acquaint their children as much as possible with aspects of their professional lives as well as with the work they do in the home and community.

Fourth, in view of the above, I advocate *maintaining an ongoing discussion with your children about the extent and satisfaction of their work as well as yours.* As they become more intimately acquainted with what you are doing, so you should stay abreast of their work experience, whether in the home, at school, in the community, or for a church or volunteer organization.

The reason I mention volunteer work so often in this book is because it is an excellent way to show children the interdependence of the human community as well as teach them that work has many rewards besides money or grades or success. Allow your child, *encourage* him, to question himself and you frequently about the personal and social value of the work you are both doing. And if sometimes the answers to those questions, yours or his, are difficult, then ponder the questions anyway and consider how the inadequacy of the answers may lead you or him to realign or alter certain aspects of your work-life.

Pleasure is as important in work as it is in love, but perhaps not so clear-cut. If work is merely what you do to survive, the pleasure element may be lost sight of. However, if it is understood as a basic form of human self-expression and social cohesion, then the possibility, even the need, for pleasure in work becomes clear. Simply put, if you don't enjoy the work you are doing, even in part, something is wrong. *The loss of pleasure in work is probably closely tied to a decreasing interest in the work itself and an increased concern about the goal of the work.* In other words, if a child is obsessed about getting straight A's in school, and works only with that motivation in mind, then the pleasure element in what he is doing will be steadily reduced to the point that he may develop a deep inner dislike for academic work. *In other words, pleasure is a barometer that indicates whether your interest in your work is authentic and legitimate, or whether you have an ulterior purpose unconnected with the work itself.*

Obviously, not all work is pleasurable all the time. The absence of pleasure is best seen in dull, repetitive, uncreative jobs where money is the worker's only motivation. Many dehumanizing jobs in our society need not be so if we organized ourselves and our economy more efficiently, rationally, humanely. But this is a topic for another book. In the meantime —until we change the world—it is possible, here and now and with the right spirit, to find pleasure in work.

From the perspective of history, *all* work is trivial and meaningless. Few products of human labor endure a decade, let alone a generation, let alone an age. Almost nothing lasts longer than that. With this in mind, we might acquire a certain humility and lightness of spirit that can save us from false and debilitating illusions about the indispensability and finality of our work, and enable us to derive pleasure by working simply for love of the work, of ourselves, of our fellows, or (if you wish) of God.

There is too little time in a human life for the luxury of overseriousness. We needn't fear becoming flip. *Effort, value,* and *self-discipline* (an element we'll discuss in a moment) are the heavy guns of work which ensure that human labor is not lightly dismissed. Thus, there is all the more need in our work for the pixie of pleasure, who brings lightness, perspective, viability, and tolerance.

We first encountered this spirit of play in the chapter on love, and it will be developed at length in Chapters 7 ("Play") and 8 ("Faith"), but the fact that it is involved in so many human activities, and sustains and enhances them, makes it akin to leaven in the bread of strength—not merely coping strength, but the strength of fullness as well. Lightness is the sworn enemy of obsession and illusion, and when it is present while you work, there is a strong likelihood that you are growing from your labor.

Parents should be on the lookout to create and reinforce the lightest moments of work with children. Doing the dishes needn't always be a dull nightly routine, and it won't be if the smallest effort is made to inject into it conversation, humor, song, or mirth. Similarly, homework needn't always be frustrating for the child. Spelling, arithmetic, learning a language, history, in fact almost *any* subject, can be learned with lightness, particularly if the parent participates. Good teachers know that the road to effective learning is paved with bricks of humor, wit, pleasure, joy. Jobs that bring a person in contact with the public also have built-in opportunities for pleasure. In sum, it needn't ever be hard to find pleasure in work, if the will to do so is imaginatively alive.

There are times when *pleasure* is in very short supply, and when the temptations to give up on the task mount formidably. Then *self-discipline,* the final element of work, is called for. The dictionary defines self-discipline as *"the ability to regulate oneself for the sake of improvement."* I would add that *self-discipline is what keeps you going when no other element of work can.* Not all work requires self-discipline, but the kinds that do are usually those with the greatest potential for providing long lasting worth.

Self-discipline is what replaces the euphoria of the honeymoon beginning of work. It's what ensures the development of habits and patterns, the acquisition of technique, finesse, experience, and confidence, which are absolutely essential in many kinds of work. To become self-disciplined, a child must understand and accept the fact that some of the most significant experiences of love, work, and play are not easily had, but result from long hours of patient planning, preparation, execution, failure, and recommencement.

Self-discipline and effort, by the way, are not the same thing. The former is harder because it is needed in many situations where the rewards are not immediate—the training needed to become a fine pianist, for example, or a fluent speaker of Russian, or a good carpenter. Effort without self-discipline will become erratic and perfunctory. It will lose the full exercise of the personality, the imagination, the intelligence, and the dexterity which self-discipline demands and provides. Self-discipline, in sum, ensures *that you are fully committed* every time you sit down at the piano bench or before the desk or easel.

In areas of work where self-discipline is required of a child, it is best if you, the parents, are nearby. Your role need not be active and interventionary, but while the hard lessons of self-discipline are being learned your presence is reassuring and encouraging. The parents' confidence in the child gives him the confidence he needs until he can develop it for himself.

For example, I try to be present in the background every once in a while when my children are having a piano or tennis lesson or when they are doing their homework. I also try to drop by every so often to their places of work in the community. In other words, self-discipline is learned alone, but the experience need not be lonely. Self-discipline draws heavily on commitment, by the way, which takes us back to Chapter 4 ("Responsibility"). Commitment becomes decisive in a work situation that demands self-discipline. The plan, and the child's commitment to it, are initially somewhat artificial supports, as is the parent's occasional presence. They lend confidence and discipline to the child until he can supply the prefix "self-" to these words.

In Chapter 3 we discussed love as something more than warm feelings and ready affection, necessary as these are; and in this chapter we have discussed work as something more than a means of survival, crucial as this is. We defined love *actively*—in terms of time spent with people in *effortful, valuable, pleasurable, disciplined* ways. It is no mere coincidence that *these same categories and criteria apply to work. For love and work are the key expressions not only of every human personality, but also of our interaction with each other.* Love, in a very real sense, is a kind of work that we do *with* people—most intensively with certain special people, but also with people in general. Similarly, in the last analysis, work takes on meaning and provides worth to an individual as it relates a person to other people and the betterment of human life in society.

In other words, love and work are opposite sides of the same coin. They are both active expressions that interrelate precisely because they lie at the heart of man's relationship to his fellows. At the same time, while both complete themselves in man's relationships with other men, they start out from the

center of a separate personality. Hence, curiously, both run
the risk of becoming self-centered, self-glorifying, self-destructive. To avoid this risk and to best express this personal center,
love and work must relate to other centers and to new considerations and dimensions beyond the self and human society.
In other words, as the strength which flows from mature loving
and working is assimilated, we leave the realm of coping and
begin to approach the higher altitudes of the strength of fulfillment. The next two chapters—*Play* and *Faith*—will attempt to
explore the mountain "above the timberline."

CHAPTER 7

Play

A child's world is fresh and new and beautiful, full of wonder and excitement. It is our misfortune that for most of us that clear-eyed vision, that true instinct for what is beautiful and awe-inspiring, is dimmed and even lost before we reach adulthood. If I had influence with the good fairy who is supposed to preside over the christening of all children I should ask that her gift to each child in the world be a sense of wonder so indestructible that it would last throughout life, as an unfailing antidote against the boredom and disenchantments of later years, the sterile preoccupation with things that are artificial, the alienation from the sources of our strength.

Rachel Carson

The original draft of the manuscript for this book did not include a separate chapter on play, which is itself an interesting comment on the degree to which even critical people may be influenced by the reigning ethic of a society. Without much thought on the matter, I assumed play would fit as a subtopic in some other chapter. This casual near-decision sadly reflects the attitude of American society, which subordinates play to more "serious" matters. Fun, leisure, sport, "a good time" are of course much talked-about and indulged-in activities. Indeed, whole industries thrive on them. But the play element in

its deepest, truest sense has been forgotten, corrupted, or repressed in our culture.

Play no longer has any organic tie to our civilization, which
is why we treat it as an adjunct to "more important" things,
like work. However anachronistic it may seem, we still live in
a society that is spiritually affiliated to the work ethic of industrial capitalism, a world of inverted priorities where, it has
been said, "one does not work to live; one lives to work." The
irony is that this remains our state of mind even though the ac-
tual economy and society which created it have evolved. Since
the Second World War people in ever-increasing numbers are
finding increasing amounts of free time, but the sad fact is they
don't know what to do with it.

What is play? *True* play is *both* an activity and an attitude.
More precisely, play is an activity which gives rise to a won-
derfully strengthful attitude of mind. As an activity, play is as
wide-ranging and varied as the manifestations of culture itself.
There are games of chance, games of skill, the play of mimicry
and simulation, and the play of dance and frolicking. Everything from roulette, chess, cops-and-robbers to whirling and
sliding, solitaire, and the decathalon counts as play. Generally,
however, looking over the entire field, it is possible to stake
out five formal characteristics:

First of all, true play is *free*—freely chosen and unobliga-
tory. As soon as coercion or requirement enter the picture, the
nature of play becomes marred. The attractive and diverting
qualities of true play are lost. This is a common occurrence in
our society. I know of one mother whose ambitions for her son
obliged the lad to spend hours a day in the pool training to become a great swimmer. For a number of years the boy acceded
because he felt he had no choice, but he grew to hate swimming and gave it up when he got away from his mother's control. A friend of mine who is a swimming coach once said to
me, "I'd like to coach a team of orphans." And I know what
she meant.

Second, play must be *separate* from everything else. It has to exist within its own time and space, possess its own rules and conventions, set up its own boundaries and order, and create its own course, meaning and illusion. (Indeed, the root of the word "illusion" comes from the Latin *in-lusio*—which means "in play.") Pretending is therefore a major sustainer of play, especially child's play. Pretending may be taken very seriously. I remember once when my daughter Dorothy was two or three. We had decided to move to another neighborhood, and Dorothy hated to leave because she had made friends with some older children across the street. The day before we left, one of these children came to my wife Hester and said sadly, "We're so sorry that you're moving now, Mrs. Ford, just when Dorothy's 'pretender' is starting to work good."

Another touching example of the importance of pretending to kids was supplied by the Dutch writer Johan Huizinga in his classic study of play (*Homo Ludens*). A father came home one evening from work and went to greet his six-year-old son who was playing on the furniture in the dining room. The son had arranged the chairs in a long chain and was seated on the first one, pretending to be both the engine and the engineer. He was so deeply engrossed in his play that when the father leaned over to kiss him, the boy whispered in his ear, "Don't kiss the engine, Daddy, or the carriages won't think it's real!"

Third, play is *unproductive*. In other words, it is its own justification. It has very little to do with the other functions of life—e.g., harvesting crops, improving national security, or having children. But if play is unproductive, it is not pointless; for although it serves no ulterior goal in the "real" world, play is vital to producing the sort of strength and health that underlie and enhance much of what we do and are. Sand castles on the beach are functionless; they will be destroyed by the flood tide. But who's to say that in the life and satisfaction of an architect or painter or builder the sand castles of his childhood were pointless?

Play is thus like prayer: it exists for itself. In the next chapter we shall see that the play attitude is more profoundly related to prayer than simply as a metaphor. The kind of strength and health that true play inspires in a life will indeed reach into all areas of that life; but as with the strength that comes from loving God, this strength and health can only be received if play is done for its own sake.

Fourth, play should be *undetermined*. Its course and results need not be known beforehand. In other words, the process of play ought to leave space for players' improvisations and initiative which (except in games of pure chance) will influence the outcome. The undetermined, improvisational character of play, even games, is crucial for children—more so, in fact, than scrupulously adhering to a game's conventions, and this is so because playing is far more important than winning in the creation of strength.

As a probation officer at a juvenile detention home in Ohio, I got to know one of the attendants—a sensitive, caring man who had an uncanny knack for getting through to kids. I used to watch him work with the tough, almost inaccessible teenagers from the inner city of Cleveland. The man's methods were unconventional but successful, and they illustrate the indeterminate element of play activity at its best. One day he was working with a teen-ager who had been arrested for homicide. The boy was unapproachable by nearly everyone else on the ward. They played chess, which the boy had elected to do, but it soon became apparent that the teen-ager had his own rules for the game. My friend went along with the new conventions, and soon the boy was engrossed in the play. He was engrossed because he was using his own intiative, was improvising in his own way. Obviously, this sort of thing happens rarely, but it might happen more often with all children, and happen more beneficially, if the *indeterminate* and *improvisational* character of play were permitted equal, sometimes superior, status with conventions and winning.

Finally, play should be *fun*. It should arouse excitement, happiness, wonder, laughter, and joy. Play is profoundly *non-*

serious, though not *un*serious, and its course should elicit spontaneity, abandon, and release.

Play, in short, may not be serious, but it is critical—very much so. At its best it is a rich and integrative experience that nourishes and synthesizes such varied talents and states of mind as freedom, discipline, inventiveness, detachment, fantasy, solitude, and group spirit. Under the right circumstances play can do all these things unobtrusively and relatively unaided, requiring and asking no great effort from the child and no intervention from the parent. For our purposes, the child's frequent participation in true play as an activity will foster in him the *play attitude of mind and the strength that flows from it.*

Play attitude is harder to define than play activity, because it is more abstract and far-reaching—indeed, it can inform nearly all the thoughts, words, and deeds of a person and may figure in almost all the cultural manifestations of a civilization, from language and war to poetry, law, sports, and politics. *The play attitude is a disposition or confidence of mind that allows a person to enjoy what he is doing without feeling compulsive about it.* It frees a person from stress and gives his life perspective by injecting lightness, humor, and transcendence into all his activities.

Take the compulsive grade-grubber who has no time for relaxation and play, and no play attitude to sustain him. His compulsiveness may stand him in seeming good stead until a crisis comes along—say, a bad grade or two in spite of his efforts. At this point the accumulated force of unleavened compulsiveness and seriousness could overwhelm the child's defenses and break his spirit. In the moment of stress he may crack—react with fury, or despairing self-doubt, or depression, or (most commonly) endless rationalizations and excuses. There will be no reserve of humor to enable him to laugh through the tears and anger, no perspective that will frame the event in question and minimize it, no inner detachment to insulate the child's precious cargo of soul, heart, and morale from infection by the germs of frustration in a competitive society. The youngster will be at the mercy of his blind commitment to grades, and his successes will be merely brittle mock-strengths masking inner weaknesses.

All of this is not to say that playfulness is fundamentally an attitude of frivolity or unseriousness, though it may well have moments of fancy, comedy, and laughter. *Play is greater than seriousness because it can include and transcend seriousness.* A child with the strength of the play attitude would be no less surprised or irritated by a bad grade than the compulsive youngster would be, and he certainly would be no less serious about the quality of his work and endurance of his effort, but in the crunch of disappointment he would not be victimized by his seriousness, because he would be able to surmount it. The play attitude contains seriousness, but it contains a lot more as well. The effect of this attitude in a young person's life is to nurture an inner space, untrammeled and unharassed by the demands of life, where joy, peace, freedom, pointlessness, and fun can be had for nothing.

The catch in all of this is that there is a yawning chasm between what play could be or used to be, and what it currently is. Our basic mistake is that we have made play into a kind of work instead of keeping it autonomous and worthy by itself, or, better, instead of letting play infuse work, as we saw in Chapter 6. The most distinguishing quality of play—its separateness from the world of seriousness, production, the everyday—is in danger of being lost.

Take organized sports. We have systematized, regimented, and invested in them to a point where they are now a major national industry dominated by the media, the middlemen, the professionals, and the financiers. The spirit of the professional has little to do with the play spirit. For him and those who live off him, play is a job, pure and simple; it lacks joy, spontaneity, carelessness.

The same holds true for sports equipment. It, too, has become a big business which strongly influences the consumer population through advertising. More and more, as a people, we tend to associate play with expensive products, with expensive trips to resorts, and with expensive lessons from professionals. The athletic shoe manufacturers, for instance, appear to be trying to subordinate the Olympics (and the Olympic champions) to selling their products. From a different angle, the politicization of the Olympics has further introduced the real world into what has always stood as the great festival of international play—to the detriment of both worlds.

Play, Johan Huizinga wrote, should and can be a fountain of culture, as it was for the ancient Greeks. The ancients realized better than we that freedom, leisure, play are fundamental to the fulfilled life; are, indeed, superior to work, whose main function should be to provide opportunity for play (and should itself derive enrichment and greater efficiency from play). Aristotle, for example, saw the play spirit as the center of culture. "We are unleisurely only in order to have leisure," he wrote.

But today we have rearranged and inverted these priorities. As a society we have lost touch with spontaneity, joy, lightness, improvisation, and humor as the springs and sources of culture, and in their place, we have only seriousness, regimentation, system, growth, profit, material. In place of true play we have developed any number of inadequate surrogates —what the Romans used to call "bread and circuses." Indeed we are fairly strangling in our leisure machines; we straitjacket ourselves and our children with organized sports and competition. We bedizen the landscape with gaudy amusement parks, luxurious campsites, the plush inessentials of a Hilton hotel, and massive stadiums and arenas where we stage our own variety of gladitorial contests; yet we are like starving men who don't know how to eat surrounded by banquets. We are a nation of leisure, a people cowed and cajoled into making fun the strenuously sought-after goal of our lives; yet we know so little about true play.

The young suffer most from this weakness in our culture, for the young are those to whom play comes most naturally and instinctively. For them we have made play into a caricature of itself by isolating one genus of play—the competitive— and converting it into the whole species. We have invaded their fantasy life with our work-oriented frets over winning, organizing, scoring, succeeding, becoming expert. "Go practice your swing until it's perfect." "You gotta *work* at your ground strokes before they can be great." And the most common, wearisome bromide of them all: "Son, anything worth doing is worth doing well." Surely there should be one day a week when G. K. Chesterton's reversal of that faulty wisdom is honored: "If a thing is worth doing at all, it is worth doing badly." In other words, a time must be set apart when the demands of the work conscience do not hold uncontested sway; a time when excellence, success, and winning are not the sole motivations; when fantasy, improvisation, celebration, and even folly and whimsy have their day.

I am reminded of a recent film, *Bad News Bears,* which illustrates these points. The film is about a middle-aged, ineffectual, itinerant pool cleaner (Walter Matthau) who consents, for the money in it, to coach twelve or fifteen utter losers into a functioning baseball team. Precisely because the boys are absolutely no good, they operate in a kind of free, demilitarized zone, outside the frighteningly competitive encounters between the other warring teams in the league. This suits Matthau very well, because he feels only contempt and indifference for the whole ethos of winning and the cruel and inhuman means the other coaches employ to win. But Matthau accomplishes his job too well. By bringing in two cracking good outsiders, one of whom is a girl pitcher (Tatum O'Neal), Matthau turns the Bears into contenders for the championship. And best of all, he does it *his* way, replacing the customary browbeating and anxiety-mongering of Little League with the joy of playing and closeness of team spirit.

Then, during the final game, Matthau's desire to win sud-

denly leads him momentarily to betray the spirit and joy that
he and his Bears have built up over the weeks. He orders his
crackerjack outfielder to catch all the flies, even when it means
poaching on his teammates' terrain, and he orders another
player to step into the pitcher's throw so he can take a free
base. The Bears are astonished and hurt by this reversal in
their coach's treatment of them, but they can do nothing.
Matthau, however, catches himself when he sees his rival
coach slap and degrade his pitcher, who happens also to be the
man's own son, because the boy is not doing well. Matthau
comes to his senses, throws in his second string at the crucial
point, blows the game, but saves the day because in the clutch
he stood by his boys and their trust.

Little League, as we all know, is a flawed American institu-
tion. Most professional ball players wouldn't let their sons get
near Little League, precisely because too often the experience
is strength-depleting, not strength-enhancing, for children.
*When the human beings involved in play, or the joy that de-
rives from the play, become of secondary importance to winning, the strength potential of the play activity is lost.*

The occupational hazard of any kind of child's play is that
it lends itself to all manner of extraneous baggage—competitiveness, vicarious parental involvement, social status, profes-
sionalization, exploitation, etc. When it does, the delicate
nature of real play—selflessness, timelessness, goal-lessness—is
injured, perhaps lost. Playing with children in the right way is
essential. Any game will do—from chess to ice hockey to tid-
dlywinks, or the fantasy play of your own creation, or romping
or dancing. It's all suitable grist for the strength-building mill.
The shared fun, laughter, and amusement contribute mightily
to the child's strength.

Playing with your child, however, may not be as easy as it
seems. The boredom and idleness that lead many children to
turn on the TV are pathetic illustrations of their inability to
play. Though many children may resent and resist the demand

to work and to succeed, they often do not even care about play, indeed may not know how to play. The freedom from constant striving, the chance to step entirely outside the psychic ethos of the work-world, puzzle and disconcert many young people. The improvisation, abandon, apartness, apparent wastefulness and goal-lessness of true play are neither congenial nor comprehensible to children bound by the mentality of winning.

Planned vacations, scheduled lessons, meets, contests, recitals, and matches, organized excursions to Disneyland—*these* are things that young people understand and depend upon. These are the play-surrogates of the work-world, in whose absence the youngster knows only how to fall back on TV or movies or congregating with his peers for the purpose of doing nothing, because none of them knows how to play either.

I remember my son John's first trip home after he had been away at school for many months. In his absence another generation of young people—his little brothers—had taken over the house. Walking into the children's area of our home, commonly known as the family room, and gazing out the windows to the adjoining back yard, John took in the comparative emptiness of room and yard (only the TV set was in use) and asked, "Where are the tree forts, the erector sets, the Lincoln logs and tinker toys? Jeez, what do kids *do* these days?" To quote Thomas More in *A Man For All Seasons,* I was "well-rebuked."

Society no longer provides children with much opportunity or encouragement to develop their natural play impulse. It teaches them sports and games aplenty, and suffuses their lives with the spirit of organized competition, and the love of passive mass entertainment, but precisely because the smoke of the work ethos clings to these things, children derive very little true pleasure or strength from them. In the margins and interstices of our children's planned lives, when, for an afternoon or evening, the expectations and appointments of the adult world are temporarily suspended, young people may suddenly encounter the restlessness and bafflement of "free" time. They will try to assuage the pain of their boredom and weakness in the mental embalming fluid of the TV set. In its own pathetic way, television is the best form of play these kids have. It gives to many of them the only feeling of apartness (though distorted and inadequate), loss of self, and fantasy they will ever know in the absence of true play.

The revolt of the young people in our culture is no longer a recent phenomenon. The hippies and flower children, the yippies and Moonies, the Jesus Freaks have all been noted and analyzed at great length in books and articles. Rather than try to recount all the reasons for their burgeoning numbers, I would like to offer one somewhat overlooked explanation: more than politics or the war in Vietnam or economic injustice, what motivated whole segments of our youth to turn against the world of their parents and strike out on their own was the *search for the missing play element of culture.* Or, put differently, war and injustice struck many youth of the late-sixties as only the most blatant evils of a society without play, without respite or surcease from the omnipresence of striving, work, competition, growth, and the compulsive mentality that fostered and issued from these things.

The countercultures these young people created were an understandable and, in some instances, laudable and attractive alternative to what they had known. The love beads and long hair, the colorful clothing and flowers, the attempts at communal living and the widening of the nuclear family, the sit-ins and love-ins, the forgetting of titles, degrees, and even last names were largely good. The festivity and celebration of a concert like Woodstock, with its almost sacred and ritualistic air, constituted a true rediscovery and restoration of the play element of an earlier preindustrial era. At best there was a lightness, spontaneity, and joy in the countercultures which stood as gay rebukes to the gray-flannel world outside.

Unhappily, however, these long-forgotten qualities of true

play turned out to be nearly as strange to the young people who had dropped out as they were to the rest of us. Unfortunately, it is not possible for a society or a segment of society to change quickly and radically. The countercultures too often betrayed in mirror images the same compulsiveness, conformism, and overseriousness they were reacting against. If the caricature of true play that ordinary American society had fostered was the strangling ubiquity of competition and striving, then the countercultures got caught up in their own special corruptions and extremes. The desire to rediscover a lost ecstasy and abandon became a compulsive, addictive dependence on drugs; the wish for fantasy and momentary loss of self became in many cases lasting alienation, sometimes schizophrenia; the hope to go beyond narrow and unregenerate rationality led to mindless superstition, a naïve and sometimes dark fascination with magic, possession, the diabolic, the esoteric, the violent, and the secretive. What was good and wonderful about Woodstock for some degenerated into the pathology of the Mansonites and the Moonies.

In short, the mark of Cain is not so easily washed away as we might hope. A fitting epitaph for the countercultures' compulsive search to be free of compulsiveness is Bertolt Brecht's quotation about revolutionaries: "Alas, those of us who would prepare the ground for friendliness could not ourselves be friendly."

Is there, then, no hope at all? Is true play irretrievably lost to contemporary civilization? Are there no practical measures to be taken that could help parents and children to find a navigable route between the extremes of gray-flannelism and the Manson gang? I think there are, or I wouldn't have included a chapter on play in this book. But it has been necessary to state the problems and the real nature of play—both as an activity and an attitude—so that no misconceptions remain to frustrate the possibility of reviving true play and the strength that comes from it.

There are two great practical keys for success in cultivating play as an activity and as an attitude in your child. The first is to sculpt out a congenial psychological and temporal environment for play. Are times and places *set aside* for play? And is the atmosphere that reigns there conducive to freedom, to stepping out of the mundane? Are fantasy, whimsy, silliness, and other pointless but significant activities of true play welcome here?

Second, for play to become truly meaningful in a young person's life he will need the companionship of adults—parents, teachers, friends—who can share the excitement of the experience with him. Soon, almost simultaneously, he will need to play with other children as well, but this cannot replace, nor is it initially so decisive as, the parents' strong support and involvement with their child's play from his earliest age.

Setting aside time and space is obviously basic, particularly in the beginning when the play attitude has not yet permeated the household to the point that nearly *any* moment may be appropriate for playfulness. There has to be a dependable, recurring segment of time when adults and children in a family may play—i.e., temporarily suspend all thought of work, expectation, goal-orientation, striving, etc. It is best to do this on a daily basis—a "children's hour," in the words of Longfellow—but surely it must be done at least once a week. The child, in other words, must know that you the parent regard play as so vital that nothing short of emergency or tragedy can interfere with it. Only then will he gradually come to see that play does not necessarily follow work in the system of priorities. Only then will he start to see that play is not merely a question of games, TV, mass spectacles, trophies, equipment, winning; but that it is something far more special, more valuable than these things and very different from them.

In addition to being valued and dependable, play time must also be flexible. Flexible not only as to when it occurs, potentially anytime, but flexible as to its content and structure. Play should be allowed to happen when the child is alone, for instance. Many young children can become enraptured in their world of make-believe. My son Luke, age nine, has all his life possessed the extraordinary talent of being able to create and enter his own fantasy world nearly anytime—in a car on a long trip, at night in the family room with all of us together, alone in his own room. Luke's vivid imagination works (I should say *plays*) constantly, and sometimes it is best to permit it to happen by itself. In other words, stay open to the best mode of accommodating your child's desire to play. Sometimes it will mean leaving him alone, sometimes being with you, sometimes with friends.

Also stay flexible about play content. Play may mean going to a baseball game or taking the children and their friends to the beach. It may mean taking an extended holiday together. But these are special events, and as important as they are for variety and excitement, they don't happen often enough, nor are they sufficient by themselves, to convey the deepest sense of play to children. In the beginning especially, when the children are very young, play content should not emphasize organized competitive sports and games or expensive trips and equipment. These things can overwhelm them and become all play in their eyes, if they don't have a firm basis from their earliest years in the everyday, strength-building play of fantasy, laughter, togetherness (or solitude), creativity and improvisation, and goal-lessness.

I can offer no better example than the contrast between the months of June and July at our summer cottage in Michigan. June is a month before most families arrive on the little peninsula. It is a month when the kids must make their own fun and define their own play. What invariably happens, year in and year out, is that after some initial griping ("Gee, Dad, there's nothing to do up here"), my children busily go about making the most of the sun, water, woods, beach, and other natural attractions of northern Michigan. We are all of us busy from morning to night, sometimes together, sometimes by ourselves, sometimes having fun, sometimes doing chores or working—but the attitude of playfulness permeates all our activity and being.

Comes July. Sports are organized; games and lessons are scheduled; the young people are divided into groups by ages; adults sign up for their adult tournaments and contests; the scheduled round of cocktail parties commences for the grownups, and kiddy parties for the youngsters. Points are given, competition takes hold on the minds and hearts of children and parents alike. Everyone knows that at the end of the month a highly anticipated trophy ceremony will take place in which people's lives will be "made or unmade" by the presentation of awards and prizes. The American Reign of Competitive Fun begins to dominate the delicate spirit of playfulness that was June.

It is especially hard on young people who are not joiners and strivers, who choose to march to the beat of their own drums and enjoy their own kind of play. My son Nelson is one such young man. He resented the change from June to July. He spent one summer roaming the woods alone or with his friends looking for snakes, building cages for them (or carrying them in his shirt pocket), reading about snakes at the local library, and proudly presenting a snake circus for anyone who would come.

July for Nelson was a mockery of fun. He saw early on what it took many of the other kids longer to realize: the organized competition of July didn't have much to do with play at all, whether you won ribbons or not. It was, in the words of one of my daughters, "a kind of schooltime in the summer, Dad."

The lessons and strengths of responsibility, discipline, and work are basic to anyone who expects to cope and to experience some satisfactions. Beyond these basics, though, are higher forms of strength which create wholeness and fulfillment in life; and in this perspective, play stands very high. If the air seems rarefied, it is not because play is hard (*hard* is precisely what it shouldn't be!), but rather because it is foreign to us. A good bit of reorientation will be needed before the real thing can become part of our lives.

And we need it very badly, for play is a great deal, after all. "For many years the conviction has grown upon me that civilization arises and unfolds in play," wrote our philosopher friend Johan Huizinga, and he meant by this that the intensity and absorption of play, the detachment of the play attitude, are *primordial qualities* of what could, should, and periodically does constitute human culture. By "primordial," we mean that play stands very near the center of and radiates outward, touching all activity, thought, and relationships with which it comes in contact. Work may indeed be necessary to keep a body and soul together, to keep the roads maintained and the lights functioning in a society; but an individual life, as well as the larger culture of which it is part, are measured by the activities and satisfactions which fill the space that work creates. In other words, we work in order to live. *But how, then, do we choose to live?*

Aristotle put the question a little differently in his *Politics.* The principal issue for men, he said, is this: With what kind of activity is man to occupy his leisure?

For too many of us today, children and adults alike, *work— or the work mentality—is what occupies our leisure.* We never stop striving. There is no space which our work creates that isn't filled with more work, even if it is fun or play disguised as work. We have forgotten—indeed, we may never have known— that life was meant to serve a higher purpose than the accumulation of material success and power. There are greater strengths than the strengths of work, as important as they are. And the strength of play is greater because it transcends work without destroying or minimizing it. Play builds on work; it takes the time and opportunity that work supplies and permits men to enjoy and partake of other, higher pursuits.

This may surprise those who think life has no other purpose than work. To them, I say: the play attitude can relieve the intensity of work and thereby contribute to work's efficiency and excellence. Play goes arm in arm with the pleasure dimension of work (see Chapter 6) or the lightness and transcendence of faith (see Chapter 8). Indeed, work pleasure can be defined as the presence of a disposition to playfulness in work. In a spirit of lightness and humility, the play attitude reminds a person of his limitations and the limitations of work seriousness. Nothing in the world of work is so serious, or so wrong, or so unsuccessful (or, on the other hand, so successful and so right) that it should take control over a human life. Nothing is so serious or so wrong that detachment, humor, and playfulness need be suspended; for if they are, they will inevitably be replaced by despair or irrationality. More often than not, the best kind of work is work that is accomplished free of coercion and compulsion in an atmosphere that is relaxed. No work is so serious that an inner attitude of playfulness wouldn't add to its efficiency and excellence.

But here I go again, implicitly subordinating play to the cause of work, when this is precisely what I have been criticizing in society at large! I have spoken of the higher purposes and pursuits of life that lie beyond work. I have several times compared play to prayer or to the love of God. The classical Greeks understood well the intimate tie between festivity, celebration, and play, on the one hand, and religion and worship, on the other. As we in the twentieth century have relegated play and faith to the edges of our culture, we have neglected this relationship between the activities and the extraordinary, yet profoundly human, strengths that come from both. In love and work we discover dimensions that suggest qualities of transcendence, of strength beyond the mere ability to cope. Play and faith are activities which, if restored and reconnected in our society, can stimulate and nourish true *arete*, true excellence and fullness of strength as we discussed it in Chapter 1. Such was the intention of the original Olympian and Pythian games, whose spirit lay nearer the temple than the stadium. Indeed, far from the relatively narrow, politicized, and debased quadrennial pseudo-events which we call "Olympics," their classical namesake permitted a wide-ranging display of many kinds of strength in an atmosphere of worship and festivity.

Concluding this chapter and keeping in mind the strengths of the play attitude—*detachment, lightness, humility, awareness of pursuits beyond work, and an openness to joy, spontaneity, and abandon*—we can move on to a discussion of faith. Indeed, these strengths are the foundations of faith. Ultimately, play's closeness to faith is that it recalls to people the folly of taking themselves too seriously. Finally we are creatures of God, and He alone, to quote Plato, "is worthy of supreme seriousness." Man is only "God's plaything, but that is the best part of him." In the last analysis, the strength of the play attitude is therefore that it holds a child's heart and mind open and available to transcendence.

CHAPTER 8

Faith

When other helpers fail and comforts flee,
Help of the helpless, oh abide with me.

Henry F. Lyte

In a book about building strength in young people—or in adults, for that matter—to leave out organized religion would not be hard to do. Indeed, it would be less difficult than finding a way to include it. The tragedy of organized religion in our day, and probably in *any* day, is that it so often alienates and misleads the people of God. Mankind's problem is not so much belief, per se; the problem is the churches. It is unfortunate that the cargo of faith has so often been transported in the vessels of official religion; even so, perhaps this sad inevitability may give rise to good. Many of the most sincere, clear-headed Christians are people who, having been raised in a straitjacket of religious conformity, have gone through a painful period of rejecting the husk of religion in order to discover later *for themselves* the kernel of true faith.

Organized churchdom aside, however, there is no way of discussing strength and its creation without finally confronting what Tolstoy called the most accursed of questions, because it never stopped bothering him: *faith*. Slowly, methodically, in the course of this book, we have built a tower of strength with the traditional granite blocks—choice, love, responsibility, discipline, work, and play—that have sustained mankind and nourished our humanity from the moment our cave-dwelling forebear asked himself the question, "Who am I?" At each story of the tower, before the block could be moved into place, it had to be cleaned with a sandblaster to recover its true luster and meaning. We have reached the summit now, but before genuine faith can be seen for the great centerpiece it is, it, too, must be cleaned of the corruptions and accumulations, both religious and secular, which have limited its power to help people.

The blocks of the tower not only carry strength and meaning in themselves, they also point beyond. As love and work originate in the individual and seek to express his uniqueness, they find even greater fulfillment and meaning to the degree that they integrate the individual into the society, service, and love of his fellow men. Each of these two steps along the way—the expression of the self and the integration of the self with others—is crucial to fostering strength in a human being.

With play, we came explicitly to the threshold of a third step, from which the greatest strengths of coping *and* fulfillment are derived—and which, indeed, in a sense underlie the effort and possibility of the first two steps. The final step, the most serious yet the lightest, is the discovery of the faith which has sustained you all along—the faith whose source is beyond you, the individual struggler, even beyond your work, love, and hope for your fellow men.

Faith is the veneration, love, and trust you give to the source of ultimate meaning of your life. Many people don't reflect very carefully on their faith or its object, but their faith is there anyway; deposited in a number of underground vaults of family, loved ones, ambitions, ideals, organized religion, etc. From deep within these subterranean repositories the object of a person's faith radiates outward, strongly influencing all his values, goals, motivations, actions, thoughts, and words.

Indeed, one could say that the object of faith is the *source* of all other meanings in a person's life.

The capacity for faith is innate in all human beings, from the most skeptical to the most credulous. Everybody, whether he realizes and admits it or not, attributes ultimate meaning to something. It is vital in raising children to know what the ultimate meaning of life is for you. There is no better way to know yourself or to create strength in your children than to reflect on the ultimate meanings of life. Everyone should have an idea of what god or gods he worships; indeed, it may surprise you to learn that your gods aren't those you thought they were or should be. To avoid confronting the deepest meaning of life is easy enough to do. Many people avoid it for years until a severe crisis happens and they discover that their ultimate meaning is a thing of ashes that won't support them through the dark nights.

Moreover, here they are not setting a very good example for their children. Young people have an uncanny ability intuitively to sense what motivates their parents. They will know, even if you manage to fool yourself, what your ultimate meanings are, and they will gradually adopt them for themselves, for better or worse. At all events, it is important to realize that *the right sort of faith is a remarkable source of strength.* Anyone who experiences it will tell you that strength from faith is sometimes so great that it can enable a person to far exceed the limits of what he thought he could do.

Everyone has faith of one sort or other. The Christians and Jews presumably attribute ultimate meaning to the god of their scriptures. The humanist ascribes final meaning to the essential goodness and boundless potential of mankind. The agnostic intellectual finds it in the use of reason; the atheist may find it in himself; the Don Juans, in sexual conquest; the ambitious Sammy Glicks, in striving for professional success.

This is simple enough. These objects of faith are not equally valid or strength-producing, however. The faith of Glick and Juan seems obviously misplaced because lust, be it concupiscent or capitalist, cannot long serve as the ultimate meaning for a human being. Eventually, the man or woman who worships these gods will realize they are merely idols. Yet thousands of people pay daily or nightly devotions to such gods. It is a temptation to all of us sometimes.

It is equally clear that the worshiper of self (the atheist) is bound to be disappointed. Faith in one's self is common in our time; it mixes well with the individualist myth of American society. Obviously a certain degree of belief in self is essential in order to achieve strength—in much the same way that love and work originate inside the person and seek to express his unique personality before they move him into wider social expression. But faith-as-ultimate-meaning cannot be placed in self, because the isolated self isn't strong enough to carry the load.

Human beings are far more dependent and interdependent than they are autonomous. This may not be the way we want things, or imagine them to be; but it is the way they are. From cradle to grave, everyone is dependent upon his fellows, more than upon himself, for survival, security, skills, knowledge, identity, meaning. The very activities that infuse our life with the greatest strength and value—love, work, play—require us to acknowledge our interconnectedness, our social nature, our need for completion in, and support from, others, and possibly something even beyond that. Thus, while a belief in the self is necessary to produce strength, it begins to lose strength as the believer makes ultimate claims for the self that it cannot sustain.

It is less apparent, hence more important to point out, that the humanist and the intellectual may also be fooling themselves (though not as destructively or as certainly as Sam Glick and Don Juan) when they attribute final meaning to society, on the one hand, and to reason and ideas, on the other. Mind you, society and ideas certainly deserve our devotion, effort, and careful thought, but it is doubtful that society's or the human mind's potential for good can survive as a source of *ultimate meaning.*

Believers in man's infinite potential for good should take time to consider his prodigious capacity for evil. Indeed, human history offers a stronger case for believing in man's inherent evil and destructiveness than in his goodness and progress. This does not mean that the only alternative to unbounded faith in human potential is despair or cynicism—the recourse of many disillusioned humanists. A measure of realism (or realistic idealism, to paraphrase John Kennedy), coupled with a gingery fussiness about the repository of ultimate faith, can save the humanist and the intellectual from ultimate disappointment.

So far we have dealt with straightforward cases of people who put their faith in vessels of clay, and supposedly know and defend what they are doing. In real life, however, you don't often meet this kind of person. What makes the question of faith more complex is that many people—in fact, all of us at some time or other—are hypocrites. Verbally we subscribe to one set of standards or doctrines, usually something idealistic or religious, while our daily actions clearly show that we worship other gods.

Dostoyevsky, the Russian novelist who displayed such phenomenal insight into the human heart, summed it up well in *The Brothers Karamazov,* when he wrote: "It makes me mad to think that a man of great heart and high intelligence should begin with the ideal of Madonna and end with the ideal of Sodom. What is more terrible is that a man with the ideal of Sodom already in his soul does not renounce the ideal of Madonna. . . ." Thus it would be a rare (and candid) Sammy Glick who openly confesses to kneeling before the dollar sign or the corporate logo. More likely, Mr. Glick would be a pious, practicing Episcopalian. His life-as-lived and his articulated ideals would thus contradict each other. His presumed faith would not be a life-integrating and love-, work-, and play-controlling attitude, but a convenient façade or *ex post facto* rationalization for actions that manifestly diverge from his ideals.

Under such relatively common circumstances, Glick's Christian "faith" is not permitted to provide much strength in his life because the man's Sunday beliefs and ideals are at variance with his daily strivings and motivations. His Christianity disguises the real object of his faith (getting ahead), and this pursuit will eventually drive him mad for its unattainability, or disillusion him for its emptiness—or both.

Thus, Sammy's Christian faith is stripped of 90 per cent of its strength potential. Since it is only a justification for his actions, his faith cannot lead him to transcend himself; it merely underscores what is already present. His faith, divided in allegiance between church and marketplace, cannot integrate love and work, self and society, word and action, but fragments them. His formal religiosity and articulated ideals become a parody or substitute, not a source of strength. It is weakness masquerading as strength.

At all events, there is no point in getting bogged down in a refutation of the common idols and idolatries of our time. The task is fraught with the perils of self-righteousness and stuffiness. There will be many readers of this book—honest, sincere, candid, intelligent people—who may agree that faith in the God beyond idols is the ultimate source of strength, yet will stoutly maintain that the preceding discussion is too exclusive and persecutory. It is not my intention to quarrel with these readers. My point is only that many people these days ascribe ultimacy to many ideas, motivations, institutions, and false prophets which do not merit this final investiture and cannot long sustain it.

In other words, we are setting ourselves up for a long fall. In an age of crumbling traditions, values, doctrines—religious and secular—the faith sweepstakes attracts all manner of phony, risky, and otherwise inadequate contenders. Nothing less than a complete rehabilitation will render faith serviceable as *the* means, par excellence, of evoking and creating strength in young people. At its best, faith has provided man with sterling displays of courage, accomplishment, sacrifice, and transcendence. But, frankly, there are very few objects of faith that are able to infuse our life with much profound meaning or lasting strength. Our faith is the personal response evoked from us by the gods before whom we kneel, and far too often it turns out that they are merely statues fashioned after our own image. To surrender to the cheapening of faith in contemporary society and language, however, would be to sacrifice too powerful a weapon from the armory of human strength, and would be contrary to the spirit of this book.

Thus I shall proceed in this chapter to speak about the faith that provides strength, which lies beyond the comforting myths and fairy stories, the ideological claptrap, the gloomy despair and fashionable cynicism, the palliatives, the superstitions, and the other sundry idolatries of marketplace, meeting hall, seminar, salon, and (often enough) sanctuary.

It is important from the start to be candid about our own views and prejudices in this matter. Both authors of this book are struggling to be practicing Christians. Both of us have trekked through the wilderness to discover faith in God for ourselves, and have chosen to re-embrace religious practice. Tillich once wrote of the possibility of men becoming free *from* religion *for* religion—in other words, leaving behind the comforts of church for the lonely, difficult search for faith, and then returning to the church as one way, *if not the only* (or even the best) *way,* of witnessing for faith. Steve Englund and Ed Ford, though their journeys toward faith are by no means completed, are both sufficiently sure of what real faith is, and what it is not, that they dare risk themselves in active religious practice.

Nonetheless, we hesitate to write about these things partly because a number of eminent theologians (Tillich, Küng, Bonhoeffer) have already done so far more eruditely than we, and mainly because in areas like faith one can never speak

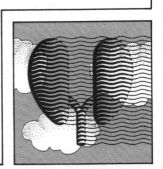

of control mind
spirit has entered body

with authority—certainly not people whose journeys are still very much ongoing. This subject is best approached confessionally, personally, open-mindedly. It is in this spirit that we shall proceed to speak of faith; for we remain convinced that it would be a deceitful omission to write about choice, love, responsibility, discipline, work, and play, and to criticize vigorously what currently passes for faith, without at least trying to describe the underlying commitment in faith which motivated the authors of this book from the start.

Assuming, then, that readers and authors agree that the right sort of faith builds strength in ourselves and our children, what are the elements of the "right sort of faith"? There are at least five dimensions of faith that seem practically and theoretically sound for judging the faith we keep and impart to our children: personal, articulable, effortful, valuable, and transcendent.

First, in order for faith to be truly strong and enduring, it must be *personal*—i.e., it must be sought for, carved out, encountered, won, discovered *on one's own.* Next to dying, faith is probably the most personal, most private activity in our lives. Each man's, each woman's, each child's, faith must suit the contours of his own mind, heart, and soul (in the sense of being his own authentic response to God's word), or it will not suffuse his life.

Finding and affirming faith is a lifelong effort, and it may happen only partially (or not at all) within the confines of an institutional church. Just as God is larger than the church, so faith in Him develops from and in a much larger circumference than religious practice. In any event, it is not a sound idea to cram organized religion down children's throats.

To expose a child to religion is fine, especially when the entire family is involved; but keep in mind that faith in God is not the same as devotion to religion, particularly for children. For them, ultimate meaning is more like the kind of love, integrity, and lived faith they see in their parents' lives. If religion is an important adjunct to the parents' faith, then it is right and good to expose children to religion, but *only* in the larger context of family love and participation. At best, organized religion may lead a young person to the water of faith, but by itself it cannot make him drink—no matter how much it frightens, coerces, or cajoles him.

Second, faith should be *articulable*—i.e., open to understanding, discussion, doubt, and change. At first glance, this may seem offensive and contrary to the very privacy and sacredness of faith, but I hope that on closer viewing the necessity of articulating faith becomes clear. Precisely because the ultimate meaning of our lives is crucially important for the way it affects other values, words, and actions, we cannot afford to leave the object of our faith in the dark. By shedding the penetrating light of comprehension on the objects of our worship, we find out whether they are really what we thought or hoped they were, and how this knowledge touches the rest of our life.

This examination can be very ticklish and difficult, because frequently the process of articulation shows us that the central meaning of our life is different from the highminded ideals and beliefs to which we pay lip service in Sunday School or in lectures to our children. A faith that is open to understanding and discussion is a faith that risks being revealed as inadequate or hypocritical; but it is also, therefore, a faith that can be changed. Discussion and doubt are not enemies of faith, but allies. They keep faith honest, keep it from degenerating into superstition, hypocrisy, self-justification, dogma, or illusion.

Articulation, understanding, doubt, and change are servants of truth, and faith must be able to withstand the light of truth, or it is not a faith that can long integrate, sustain, and direct a human life. Do not be afraid, therefore, to share your faith with your children, to discuss it and explain it to them. They, too, will learn and benefit greatly from such open-minded discussions. And if your kids press you to the wall with their questions, be glad they do, stay open, and try to answer them. For in their questions you may discover something you didn't know about your faith, or you may see ways in which you are not living it, no matter how much you talk about it. In this area, as in so many others, your children can be a Godsend.

If faith isn't *effortful,* it isn't real. Of this we can be certain. Even more than love and work, *faith requires continuous struggle and self-discipline.* Faith isn't the sort of attitude or action that life makes easy for us. All meaning, temporary or ultimate, has to be created by the person, has to be carved out of the raw stuff of his daily experiences. It doesn't just hang there, waiting to be plucked like an overripe apple. Nor is it scientifically verifiable or logically self-evident. There are many institutions, movements, philosophies, and religions eager to provide us with easy-come, effortless meanings and values; but important meanings have to be worked for, created, examined, altered, reaffirmed. *Above all, reaffirmed.* For the kind of effort that produces faith is the long-term effort of affirmation—the affirmation of our faith in the face of the chaos, mindlessness, failure, evil, emptiness, temptation, death, hedonism, decay, corruption, cynicism which constantly threaten to destroy our ultimate meanings and drive us to despair or illusion.

The effort needed to achieve real faith is what makes me question some of the religious movements—e.g., the Moonies, the charismatics, the Jesus Freaks, the Hare Krishnas, Maharaj Ji's followers, etc.—which have claimed so many young people. These kinds of cults have been around from the dawn of human history offering simple explanations, salvation, and meaning in exchange for membership and devotion. At worst, they degenerate into the authoritarianism of the Moonies or the psychopathic sickness of the Manson gang. More often, however, such groups are harmless, or even helpful in terms of obliging other social or religious or political institutions to re-examine

their own style, function, message, and faith. The charismatics
and the Jesus Freaks, for example, may have a beneficial impact on the churches in terms of reminding them of their first-
century roots and authenticity.

Nevertheless, young people who desperately seek ultimate
meaning in these movements may lose touch with the effortful
and long-range side of faith in a warm sea of mutual affection, support, ignorance, and isolation. The affirmation that
strength-producing faith requires is the affirmation of meaning
in the face of life's reality over the long haul from youth to old
age. These movements, almost by definition, shut out reality,
which is why they often hold on to their young converts for
such short periods of time. The faith-that-brings-strength may
be sparked or revitalized momentarily by a passing experience
in some movement, but over the long haul life itself is the only
arena where real faith thrives.

The *value* of faith, like love and work, is twofold: on the
one hand, its personal *value* to you, the believer, and on the
other (interrelatedly), its social *value* to your fellow men. *The
personal value of faith depends on the degree to which it sustains hope, illuminates life and world, and imparts meaning
and inspires action in the believer.* Many kinds of faith have little personal value. An ultimate belief in money or sex, for example, explains very little of life and the world; it sustains a
person only weakly, imparts narrow kinds of meaning, and
inspires only very specific and self-serving kinds of action.
Even faith in society, though it may inspire many good actions, has a hard time sustaining the believer, or imparting
meaning for him, in the event that society betrays his faith,
scorns his actions, and persecutes him. And it has no explana-
tory value at all beyond the individual and the human species.
In sum, the personal value of faith is a hard requirement to sat-
isfy. Very few kinds of faith will foot the bill.

The *social value* of faith is what connects faith with people.
In other words, the social value of your life's deepest meaning

is its capacity to radiate outward from self to society and beyond. The social value of faith, therefore, has to do with love. This is not surprising. For the authors of this book, as for the great majority of readers, love constitutes *the* critical manifestation of a person's faith.

But the love reflected from faith is a special, higher, less palpably compensated and self-oriented kind of love than we usually express or encounter. Where the social value of work rests in collaboration, and that of ordinary love in human interaction, *the social value of faith resides in service.* The reward here is far less visible and tangible, less obviously satisfying and necessary, than the rewards of love and work. But possibly for that reason, faith-inspired service is the toughest strand in the inner fiber of character. Paradoxically, the selfless service that springs from true faith is also the most self-strengthening activity. If our life's ultimate meaning, therefore, doesn't impel us to a certain degree of self-sacrifice, it isn't genuine.

Precisely because this kind of service is difficult (very few of us do it easily, quietly, gracefully), it requires the support and sustenance of a community. This is why the great traditions of religious or secular faith throughout Western and Eastern history have flourished in *community.* The denial of self that is required in the strongest, best kinds of faith is so great that the best chance of realizing it is in the company of others who are similarly motivated and believing.

Most of us never become expert at the highest kinds of self-sacrificing service; but *any parent has the opportunity to test the social value of his faith in his relations with his children.* More than most kinds of love, the love we give our children requires the invisibly rewarded, endlessly self-giving and patient attitude which flow from long-term, enduring faith. If what you need to sustain your loving actions toward your children is the immediate and constant gratification of lessons well-learned, affection and respect freely given, and understanding, sympathy, and gratitude, then believe me, you'll be frustrated and disappointed by your kids over the long haul. (And frankly, many parents *are* frustrated, disappointed, and regretful—as we'll see in the last chapter of this book.) In any event, the patience, selflessness and service we freely give our children throughout their lives will provide the best, truest model I know of for them to follow in their search for true faith.

Finally, the property most characteristic of, and most peculiar to, faith is *transcendence.* In one sense, *transcendence is the dimension of faith that pushes the believer beyond the limits of his mind, his strength, his control, his experience, and his physical state.* In another sense, *transcendence is the realization that faith is a response to and an evocation from the source of all being.* Obviously, transcendence is not an empirical, scientifically valid category; it is a mystery and will remain one. For that reason, the very nature of faith renders the whole subject difficult to speak of meaningfully unless the listener has himself experienced it.

Yet, to leave out transcendence from a discussion of faith would be to reduce faith to a subcategory of love, whereas love, in the last analysis, is surely a creation of faith. "Surely" may seem too strong to some readers; so to them I say again that this entire chapter is personal and confessional. I make no claim to speak authoritatively or exclusively, only to tell a part of the truth as I have been given the light to see it.

Transcendence is difficult to describe for a further reason: it is the one experience we have discussed in this book which deals with a quality that people can't do something about directly. For the most part, it happens *to* us, not *by* us, although I admit that one sure way to experience transcendence is to engage frequently in the kind of service I wrote about earlier in this chapter.

Transcendence is the surest sign that your faith *is* faith—i.e., that the ultimate meaning of your life is expressed by (because it infuses) your daily actions, thoughts, and words. Transcendence may happen when you feel pushed by life (or children) to the limits of your ability and endurance, when you feel drained of strength and hope, or when doubt has undermined the values and meaning in your life, perhaps even altered the words and thoughts you use to express your ultimate meaning. Then, unexpectedly and (you may feel) undeservedly, you may encounter the overwhelming presence of another strength to lean upon.

You might experience it quietly as the added drop or two of sheer grit and stamina that are needed to see you through—not dissolving your despair and hopelessness in sugary reassurance, but somehow taking these devils into itself. In other words, you may *transcend*—go beyond, surmount—the particular fix or scrap you are in and in the process of doing so you may feel the presence of a mystery, a "beyond," that is frightening and calming, controlling and loving, totally other and yet totally present.

If transcendence is the surest sign of faith, then joy is the surest sign of transcendence. For as your faith puts you in contact with the strength-beyond-strength, the experience may be accompanied by a positive feeling, like play or pleasure but much stronger and pervasive, and that feeling is joy. To the extent that it takes hold of you, you may even come to feel momentarily outside your usual state—what the mystics call *ecstasy*.

Thus we conclude what has perhaps proven to be a difficult chapter to read—heaven knows, it has been difficult to write. In the last analysis, you won't really know how strength-producing your faith is until life tests you—as it invariably does. Making the right kinds of choices, undergoing the apprenticeship in responsibility, performing the activities and self-expression which constitute love, work, and play are not achieved overnight. They originate, as we saw, in the individual self. Gradually, in time and with effort, they will lead you out into fruitful relationships with other people, and finally with the community of selves called humanity.

As this widening and expanding occur, there may come a time when the wayfarer happens upon a ground where love, work, and play themselves take root and derive being and sustenance. That ground is the ground of the best sort of faith, and from that moment forward, the discoverer's life is transformed as he suddenly realizes the source from which, and toward which, his loving and working flow. If he stays in touch with that ground, no amount of adversity or failure or disappointment in life can permanently frighten or confuse him; for the strength he derives from contact with this ground is too great and too fundamental for *anything* to prevail against it.

PART III

Hope

CHAPTER 9

Children?

"Why did you do all this for me?" Wilbur asked. "I don't deserve it. I've never done anything for you."

"You have been my friend," replied Charlotte. "That in itself is a tremendous thing. I wove my webs for you because I liked you. After all, what's a life, any way? We're born, we live a little while, we die. A spider's life can't help being something of a mess, with all this trapping and eating flies. By helping you, perhaps I was trying to lift up my life a trifle. Heaven knows anyone's life can stand a little of that."

E. B. White, *Charlotte's Web*

The question facing the authors of a book about child-rearing, and facing all prospective parents, is, *Why have children?* Few other human enterprises entail *so much* sacrifice, effort, frustration, and thanklessness in exchange for the thinnest hope of experiencing pride, satisfaction, love, and success. Raising children was never easy, but today, in a society of crumbling platitudes—when marriage itself, let alone the nuclear family, evokes hardly more interest than going to church—it may be harder, more perilous, less promising, than it has *ever* been before. Indeed, raising children is very likely the hardest thing most of us will attempt to do in our lives.

I read a dramatic illustration of the regret and bitterness

parents feel about their children in a couple of recent articles by Ann Landers. In January 1976, a young married couple wrote her to say they were undecided about whether or not to have children, and they asked the columnist to fish for reactions and opinion to the question: "If you had it to do over again, would you have children?" in the vast sea of her readership. Miss Landers printed the letter in her column[1] and instantly began netting replies by the boatload. Of the ten thousand parents, mostly mothers, who answered, *70 per cent replied, no, they would not have kids if they could choose again.*

Seventy per cent. I was staggered, and so, apparently, was Ann Landers, who wrote in a later article in *Good Housekeeping*:[2] "Twenty years of writing the Landers column has made me positively shockproof. Or so I thought. But I was wrong. The results of that poll left me stunned, disturbed, and just plain flummoxed." The writers' reasons for regretting their earlier decisions to have children varied, but the majority fell into one of three categories: parents who felt that having kids had ruined their marriage; older parents of grown-up children who felt ignored and unloved by their offspring; and the angry, bitter letters of the parents of teen-agers in trouble (usually with the law).

Subsequent polls conducted by the Kansas City *Star* and *Newsday*[3] tried to take some of the edge off Landers' shocking discovery by showing that 94 per cent and 91 per cent, respectively, said they *would* go through it all again. But these polls, between them, reached less than two thousand people, whereas Landers had five times that many respondents—and their letters were longer, more intense, and thoughtful than the usual ones she receives. In any event, whatever the exact number of regretful parents among the nearly fifty-five million

[1] Youngstown *Vindicator,* Youngstown, Ohio, January 23, 1976.
[2] *Good Housekeeping,* June 1976.
[3] *The Arizona Republic,* August 19, 1976, "Parents' Poll Result: Kids Are Worth It" by Michael Kernan, Washington Post Service.

families in this country, the stark fact remains that a lot of them include parents who are bitter and unhappy about their children. Among the many problems facing the United States, this one, though it surely doesn't get the media attention of pollution, politics, or poverty, probably disturbs more people more deeply than almost anything else, the economy included.

The first word I would say to angry parents is one of understanding and acceptance. You're damn straight: raising kids can be difficult, expensive, impossible, enervating, and thankless. Far too many married couples rushed into having children without forethought, planning, realistic expectation, and without much understanding of what the task entails. These parents were not taught the lessons involved in raising children, unless they were among the few people fortunate enough to have learned them at home. The schools and colleges of this country require far more instruction in math and history than in how to discipline kids, love them, and teach them strength, responsibility, work, faith, etc. As a result, thousands of parents are stuck in a quandary of frustration and disappointment over their kids, and not knowing how to change things.

An unhappy couple has two choices that will reduce the pain and improve matters. One is separation, and the other is to spend more strength-building time together. Parents, however, may have neither of these alternatives. Divorcing your children is impossible, and persuading them to spend more strength-building time with you may be unsuccessful.

Many parents feel locked in and desperate where their children are concerned. The only viable way out in the long run is for the parents to begin working (often unilaterally) at the hard, slow task of establishing a loving relationship with their kids, teaching them responsibility, disciplining them when necessary, teaching them work, etc.—in sum, all the difficult, but necessary things I have talked about in this book. There is no easy way out, in other words, no "free lunch" in this, or any other, serious human undertaking.

Sadly, sometimes tragically, an increasing number of parents succumb to unfortunate "choices": giving up and letting the children fend for themselves and grow up as best they can; abandoning them altogether; and, worst of all, abusing them. There are no statistics for the first choice, of course; but the figures for the next two are growing alarmingly.

A 1976 survey[4] directed by three sociologists reported results that were so dramatic that CBS News quoted them extensively in a special program on child abuse in the United States, which it aired in early 1977. The survey showed that more than 80 per cent of parents used physical punishment, including spanking, on their three- to nine-year-olds. Twenty per cent of the parents interviewed said they had at some time struck a child with some object; 4.2 per cent said they had "beaten up" the child; 2.8 per cent said they had threatened a child with a knife or gun; and 2.9 per cent said they had actually used a gun or knife on a child. In other words, of the 46,000,000 young people between the ages of three and seventeen in this country, 34,500,000 (or 75 per cent) have been physically hurt; 2,000,000 were beaten up; and 1,000,000 shot or shot at by their parents in the year 1976. Noted one of the sociologists who directed the survey, Dr. Murray A. Straus of the University of New Hampshire, these figures probably underestimate the amount of violence perpetrated in the American home. Straus's and his colleagues' findings are well summarized in the following quotation from Dr. William Welch, a syndicated medical columnist: "[T]here are signs that child abuse has so burgeoned in our troubled society that it can no longer be considered as sporadic evidence of the occasionally over-stressed. . . . Young parents, in increasing numbers these days, seemingly unable to bear what they experience as insupportable frustration, lash out at the innocent intruders on their [own] self-indulgence."[5]

[4] The *Arizona Republic*, Saturday, February 26, 1977 "Only Riots and wars top the U.S. home for violence, study finds." UPI

[5] Dr. William J. Welch, "Medically Speaking," Youngstown *Vindicator*, Youngstown, Ohio, May 24, 1976.

Honest to God, *Why have children?* And why bother to add new bodies to a world already strangling from excessive population, pollution, and nuclear proliferation? Any answer that overlooks or whitewashes the perils, difficulties, and ultimate riskiness of the child-rearing venture, and which encourages parents with idealistic platitudes about their "duty" and "obligation" to get into the kid business, would be as irresponsible as it would go unheeded. In any event, I certainly do not intend to give this kind of quick-and-easy answer to the question posed in this chapter. I trust this book, if it has done nothing else, will have impressed upon the reader the seriousness, effort, and difficulty which are inescapable in successfully raising a human family.

Is parenthood something we should avoid because it is hard and becoming harder all the time? If that is so, should we not also avoid other activities that have become increasingly difficult, some of which respresent mankind's greatest achievements (as well as failures) and are undergoing unprecedented challenge in the late twentieth century—marriage, self-government, arms limitation, and faith come to mind. Contrary to the casual expectations about life palmed off by the media and the propaganda agencies of government, society, and the economy in this country, lasting achievements in the area of human relations aren't easy. They never were—not in the twelfth century B.C., and certainly not today, when so many technological effort-savers and defenses insulate us from the reality of the human condition.

Thus, if we approach the question (Why have kids?) from the perspective of the reality of human relations, we must ask ourselves: "Is the challenge of raising children still an urgent, worthwhile, even necessary human activity?" And my answer to that question is yes. Why is my answer yes? In the last analysis, I believe we should have children for the same reason we should serve and love others—*for our own sakes.* It is we who grow and mature from raising kids; we who learn that forgetting ourselves for the sake of others helps us more than it helps them; we who grow stronger from teaching and showing strength to a child. Children need parents to grow, and adults need children for the same reason.

A celebrated author of children's books was once asked: "How do you write a book for children?" And he answered that you start by writing a book for everybody. It has been much the same kind of experience writing this book. It began as an aid to parents for raising kids, but it soon became (I hope) a book for everyone about some of the key issues and activities of human life. There are no specific rules on how to raise kids; there are only reflections upon the larger themes of life—making choices, learning responsibility, gaining strength through love, work, faith, and so on—which prove relevant to the child-rearing activity, as they prove relevant to maintaining a marriage or deepening a faith or enjoying work.

Ultimately, the only way to learn about love is to experience it. And the love demanded and taught by child-rearing is one of the great traditional embodiments of love available to men—as meaningful and relevant today as it was in Babylon or Greece. We learn love as we learn anything else—developmentally. As a young child we experience love at first narcissistically, as self-love. Through physical dependence upon our parents we learn something about object love, but we still experience love primarily as something that our parents give to us. It will be there no matter what we do.

As we grow older, if our parents love us selflessly and in strengthful ways, we gradually learn to emulate self-giving kinds of love.

In our teens we create close and intense relationships with friends of both sexes, but still, at this stage, if our loving isn't strong enough to prevail against the obstacles and threats that life throws in our path—arguments, silence, fear, insecurity, social pressure, selfishness, etc.—we have easy ways out. We can end the friendships, break up with our friends, disobey our parents.

Marriage is a major step forward in learning to love, for it commits us to a relationship where there is no easy way out, where we are obliged to give of ourselves, where we must struggle to make a go of it. The reason for the extremely high divorce rate in our society is that many young people have no idea from their previous experience of what married love is all about. Many never get beyond the self-oriented (or sexual) experience of love, and are therefore not prepared for what marriage requires.

Marriage is by no means easy, but in theory, at least, you have a mature partner who is trying with you to make the relationship work. With hard work, thoughtfulness, and some luck, the profoundly satisfying love of a good marriage can be achieved. But then what? Does the love process stop there? I think not. The love talked about in the chapter on faith is one sort of love that develops alongside of, and eventually beyond, marital love. More relevantly to this book, however, is the love that comes from raising children.

For children, like faith, offer that further dimension in the maturing process of a human being that evokes the ultimate in human outpouring—*the unstinting giving of self regardless of return.* A married couple who love one another have learned to give of themselves; but the experience of raising children will take them to a new plateau entirely. We have already touched upon the irony of this kind of self-giving—how bread cast upon the waters returns a hundredfold to him who throws it into the friendships, relationships, loves he maintains. Similarly, the special kind of friendship that raising children can bring is unique in its depth and degree of satisfaction (if also in its difficulty to create).

I use the word "friendship" purposely, for in the last, best analysis, your children *are* your friends. Indeed, your friendship with them will be one of the best results or by-products of the strength-building you have worked at over the years. Friendship, precisely because it has so few built-in rules, expectations, hazards, demands, and red tape (unlike formal marriage, family, and romantic ties), is one of the freest, purest expressions of the strength that is love.

If you understand, from the start, that children are special kinds of friends, then you'll perhaps be less insistent upon forcing them to become something they are not, upon living vicariously through them, or upon burdening them with all manner of artificial, unnecessary expectations, punishments, illusions, or demands. If you understand that your children are your friends, you'll perhaps understand sooner that the best image you can transmit to them is the image of your own, independent, consistent, giving self.

You might have children who are bright, attractive, healthy, successful; but if they are not your friends—i.e., if the love-that-is-friendship was absent from the way you raised them—then you will inevitably feel an emptiness, an ache of unfulfillment from the whole experience of child-raising. Today, in our crowded world of lonely people, when we need all the friends we can get, it is tragic to spend so much time, energy, money, and health in a venture that does not result in the abiding love that is friendship. If there is an appropriate question with which to close this book, therefore, it would be this: As you raise your children, over the long years of their infancy, childhood, and youth, are you doing things, saying things, being in ways that will cultivate and increase the possibility of friendship with them and the possibility of strength in that friendship for you both?

Bibliography

*Assagioli, Roberto. *The Act of Will.* New York: Viking, 1973.

Bonhoeffer, Dietrich. *The Cost of Discipleship.* New York: Macmillan, 1963.

Caillois, Roger. *Man, Play and Games.* Glencoe, Illinois: Free Press of Glencoe, Inc., 1958.

Erikson, Erik. *Toys and Reasons: Stages in the Ritualization of Experience.* New York: W. W. Norton, 1977.

Ford, Edward E. (with Robert L. Zorn). *Why Marriage?* Niles, Illinois: Argus, 1974.

*Ford, Edward E. & Zorn, Robert L. *Why Be Lonely?* Niles, Illinois: Argus, 1975.

*Glasser, William. *Reality Therapy.* New York: Harper & Row, 1965.

——— *Schools Without Failure.* New York: Harper & Row, 1969.

——— *The Identity Society.* New York: Harper & Row, 1975 (revised edition).

——— *Positive Addiction.* New York: Harper & Row, 1976.

*Hartshorne, M. & Holmes, M. *The Faith to Doubt.* Englewood Cliffs, N.J.: Prentice-Hall, 1963.

*Huizinga, Johan. *Homo Ludens.* Boston: Beacon Press, 1955.

Institute for the Study of Humanistic Medicine. *Dimensions of Humanistic Medicine.* San Francisco: Institute for the Study of Humanistic Medicine, 1975.

Kitto, Humphrey D. *The Greeks.* New York: Penguin, 1951.

Lewis, C. S. *Mere Christianity.* New York: Macmillan, 1964.

Pieper, Josef. *Leisure: The Basis of Culture.* New York: Pantheon, 1952.

Remen, Naomi. *The Human Patient.* New York: Doubleday/ Anchor Press, forthcoming.

Terkel, Studs. *Working.* New York: Avon, 1975.

Tillich, Paul. *The Shaking of the Foundations.* New York: Scribner's, 1948.

*Travelbee, Joyce. *Interpersonal Aspects of Nursing.* Philadelphia: Davis, 1971.

*Underhill, Evelyn. *Practical Mysticism.* New York: Dutton, 1915.

Weill, Simone. *The Need for Roots.* New York: Harper & Row, 1971.

*Books marked with an asterisk are especially recommended.